We Die Like Brothers

We Die Like Brothers

The sinking of the *SS Mendi*

John Gribble and Graham Scott

Historic England

Published by Historic England, The Engine House, Fire Fly Avenue, Swindon SN2 2EH
www.HistoricEngland.org.uk

Historic England is a Government service championing England's heritage and giving
expert, constructive advice.

© Historic England 2017

First published 2017

The views expressed in this book are those of the authors and not necessarily those of
Historic England.

ISBN 978-1-84802-369-7 (hardback)
ISBN 978-1-84802-472-4 (paperback)

British Library Cataloguing in Publication data
A CIP catalogue record for this book is available from the British Library.

The right of John Gribble and Graham Scott to be identified as authors of this work has
been asserted by them in accordance with the Copyright, Designs and Patents Act 1988.

Every effort has been made to trace image copyright holders and we apologise in advance
for any unintentional omissions, which we would be pleased to correct in any subsequent
edition of this book.

Brought to publication by Sarah Enticknap, Publishing, Historic England.
Typeset in Georgia Pro 9.5/11.75pt
Edited by Anne McDowall
Indexed by Alan Rutter
Page layout by Hybert Design Ltd, UK
Printed in the UK by Gomer Press

Front cover: Nigerian troops lounging on the hatch covers of the Mendi.
[© Imperial War Museum Q15639]

Contents

Preface

When we first engaged with the wreck of the steamship *Mendi* back in 2006, we realised very quickly that this site was something out of the ordinary: a shipwreck whose story could still speak across the generations.

The 100th anniversary commemorations of the First World War have brought with them a new and very welcome opportunity to focus on the sacrifices made by the people of many nations in that conflict, including the people of Britain's former colonies and dominions. It has also brought us the chance to retell the story of the *Mendi*; to explain why so many sons of Africa were on this ship in the bitter cold of the English Channel in February 1917; and to consider why the consequences of that night have rippled through South African society ever since.

Although this is not the first major account of the loss of the *Mendi* to be published, it is the first account to include the wreck and our current state of knowledge of the archaeology of the site in the telling of the *Mendi* story. It is therefore part of the major contribution that archaeology, funded in substantial part by Historic England, is currently making to our understanding of the role that the war at sea played in 1914–18 conflict.

As a South African, John has naturally focused on examining the role that the men of the *Mendi*, the black African men of the South African Native Labour Corps, played in that conflict, and this forms a major part of this book. As the son of a Liverpool family, it is the fact that the *Mendi* was a Liverpool ship that first drew Graham into the story and it is the story of the ship and what happened to those who sailed on it that he has focused upon. To both of us, however, the *Mendi* remains very much a story of how men treated unequally in life have eventually come to be honoured without distinction of creed, colour or rank. It is the lessons that the present and future generations can draw from this that makes this particular wreck, just one of the hundreds of First World War wrecks to be found around the English coast, so special.

John Gribble and Graham Scott
November 2016

1
Introduction

In July 2015, a new exhibition was opened at the South African National War Memorial at Delville Wood. This addition to the Memorial's museum, supported by Historic England, tells the story of one of South Africa's worst maritime disasters: the loss of the Liverpool steamship *Mendi* off the Isle of Wight in February 1917. The *Mendi* was a requisitioned troopship, built on the Clyde in 1905 when the famous shipyards were the pre-eminent force in world shipbuilding. Carrying goods and passengers, the ship was already a veteran of the trade between the great port of Liverpool and the ports of Britain's colonies in West Africa when it was requisitioned in 1916.

Steaming through the narrow waters of the English Channel, the ship was carrying troops from Cape Town to help the British Army in France. They were fearful of attack as the Germans had resumed their unrestricted submarine warfare around the British coast. However, the *Mendi* was not hit by German mine or torpedo; rather, it was sunk in the fog by another British vessel, the much larger mail ship *Darro* and its reckless captain, Henry Winchester Stump. Advancing at full speed and with little regard for the risk of collision, the *Darro* crashed into the *Mendi*, sinking it in 20 minutes and leaving hundreds of men clinging to unsuitable life rafts in the freezing cold water. In immensely difficult conditions, very few men were rescued and more than six hundred died.

The loss of the *Mendi* occupies a special place in South African military history. This is not because it remains one of the country's worst disasters at sea. Nor is it because hundreds of lives were lost or because it was a troopship. Sadly, many ships went down with great loss of life during the First World War. Rather, it is because the men it was carrying were not fighting troops and they were not white;[1] they were members of the South African Native Labour Corps (SANLC).

This Corps was part of a much wider force of men recruited from all over the British Empire and China to support the fighting troops on the Western Front and in other theatres of the war by building roads, bridges, railways and trenches and handling the enormous quantities of war supplies arriving in the ports and railway yards of France and Belgium.

Prevented from being trained as fighting troops by their own Government, the men of the SANLC hoped that their contribution to the war effort would lead to greater civil rights and economic opportunities in the new white-ruled nation of South Africa after the war. These hopes were to be dashed by white opposition and British indifference in the years that followed. In the post-war years, the loss of the *Mendi* and the sacrifice made by those who drowned therefore became a focus of resistance to white minority rule in South Africa.

Since the end of apartheid in 1994 and the advent of black majority rule, the loss of the *Mendi* has been brought officially to the fore in South Africa. An example of this is the South African national award for bravery, which is now called the 'Order of Mendi'. This is awarded to South African civilians and military personnel who have performed extraordinary acts of bravery that have involved them placing their own lives in great danger.

In 1995, in a testament to the political importance of the *Mendi* to the country, the late President Nelson Mandela invited Queen Elizabeth II to unveil a memorial at Avalon Cemetery in Soweto to the men lost when the *Mendi* sank (Fig 1.1). This was an act of great symbolic importance, given her grandfather George V's failure to ensure that the men of the SANLC received the medal that had been intended to be given to all of the participants in the First World War from the British Empire and its Dominions. The Soweto memorial is one of a number that have been erected across South Africa in the last 20 years.

Fig 1.1 Queen Elizabeth II and the late President Nelson Mandela unveil a memorial at Soweto in 1995 to the men who died on the Mendi. *[© Getty Images]*

The importance of the *Mendi* has not been lost on the South African military. They have embraced the SANLC and the loss of the *Mendi* not just as a way of redressing the lack of official recognition given prior to 1994 to the men who died on the ship but also as a means of demonstrating that South Africa's military past was multiracial and not exclusively white. One of the most powerful ships in the South African Navy has been named SAS *Mendi*, and South African soldiers, sailors and air force personnel attend commemorative events linked to the SANLC and the *Mendi* both at home and abroad. In 2012, a national Armed Forces Day to honour the men and women of the SA National Defence Force was instituted in South Africa. It takes place annually on 21 February, the anniversary of the loss of the *Mendi*.

The same desire to ensure that the sacrifices made by *all* of South Africa's people in the wars of the 20th century are appropriately commemorated lies behind the *Mendi* exhibition, part of a general reinterpretation of the museum at the South African National War Memorial at Delville Wood. Delville Wood is the site of a desperate and heroic battle fought by white South African troops during the Battle of the Somme in 1916. After the war, the battlefield was gifted to the South African people and a national war memorial was built there in the 1920s. In the 1980s, the apartheid Government added to the memorial by building a museum there that was intended to commemorate the sacrifices made by South Africans in world conflicts of the 20th century. The museum drew criticism for what was perceived to be a lack of recognition for non-white South Africans and for the way in which they were depicted, which many regarded as disrespectful. As part of the commemoration of the First World War, the museum is being redesigned and reinterpreted, with the *Mendi* exhibition being the first installation of new information.

The *Mendi* is a known shipwreck and therefore an archaeological site. The multiracial team of South African and British heritage and creative professionals who designed the *Mendi* exhibition at Delville Wood was therefore fortunate to have access to the work carried out on the wreck site.

The wreck of the *Mendi* was first identified in the 1970s by the British diver Martin Woodward, whose museum at Arreton on the Isle of Wight contains an important collection of artefacts recovered from the site, and recreational divers subsequently visited and investigated the wreck. They were followed in turn by archaeologists, alerted to the significance of the wreck by news of commemorative activities in both the UK and South Africa and a realisation that it was a wreck of unusual international significance. Designation as a Protected Place under the Protection of Military Remains Act 1986 followed, and dealt with concerns over the uncontrolled removal of artefacts from this sensitive site, and from February 2017, the *Mendi* qualifies for protection under the UNESCO

2001 Convention on the Protection of the Underwater Cultural Heritage. Although archaeological work has been restricted to desk-based research and limited geophysical survey supported by Historic England and the South African Heritage Resources Agency, the knowledge generated and the objects acquired by the work of these divers and archaeologists has enabled the exhibition to tell the story of the *Mendi* and to commemorate the men lost, from an archaeological as well as a historical perspective.

In the 100th year since the tragic loss of the ship, the wreck of the *Mendi* is a physical symbol of black South Africans' long fight for social and political justice and equality and is one of a very select group of historic shipwrecks from which contemporary political and social meaning can be drawn. While archaeological investigation is still ongoing, the emergence of an archaeological perspective has enabled this new study of the loss of the ship and of the history of the South African Native Labour Corps to be written. In the following chapters, the story of the SANLC and its place in the war effort will be examined and the current state of archaeological knowledge of the wreck will be used to reconsider what we know about the ship and the disaster that befell it and those who were on board.

2
British military labour during the First World War

The story of the *Mendi* and the South African Native Labour Corps has its roots in the British military labour structure that developed during the First World War to provide support to the Empire's fighting troops.

Early labour in wartime France

When the British Expeditionary Force landed in France on 7 August 1914, three days after the declaration of war, it did so without any formal labour component within its ranks. Traditionally, the standing army relied on its own, internal services for its logistical needs: the Army Ordnance Corps

Fig 2.1 The Army Service Corps unloading meat in Dunkirk (March 1917). [© Imperial War Museum Q4800]

for dealing with arms and munitions, the Army Service Corps for food, water and other stores (Fig 2.1) and the Royal Engineers for roads and infrastructure-related labour needs. These services were bulked up as and when necessary by sourcing unskilled labour from local areas, or through military fatigue details.[1]

The first Army Service Corps (ASC)[2] labour companies arrived in France in late August 1914 and began the task of organising the ports, setting up supply depots and arranging a system to transport the supplies that were soon to come streaming in.[3] Following army policy, and in terms of an agreement reached with the French Government in 1912, the labour required by the ASC to unload supplies at the French ports of Le Havre, Rouen and Saint-Valery was initially provided by French civilians.[4]

This use of French labour was not a lasting solution. Once it became clear that the war would not be 'over by Christmas',[5] the French labour used to unload British supply ships quickly became inadequate as France started conscripting increasing numbers of men to fight.[6] 'The colossal armies of the First World War imposed colossal – and largely unforeseen – problems ... [and] the onset of static warfare by the end of 1914 added unprecedented demands for workers to build trenches and other facilities'.[7]

As a result, the movement of stores and munitions, the repair or construction of roads and railways and the building of defences quickly fell to the British troops and rapidly became an established part of their fatigue routine. This work often took precedence over periods of rest for the infantry behind the lines and led to a decline in the physical and mental condition of the frontline troops.[8]

The situation was not ideal and, as the war escalated, the army expanded and casualties mounted, it grew increasingly untenable: more and more men were needed for the vital logistical support that was required to keep the army moving. The need for an additional, non-combatant labour force to support the fighting units was soon obvious to the War Office and it acted quickly to find a solution. By December 1914, five labour companies, each consisting of roughly 500 men, had been created within the ASC and dispatched to France.[9] Over the next two years, the military infrastructure for meeting the labour requirements in the various theatres in which the British Army was engaged expanded phenomenally.

The units created differed widely in their purpose and make-up, and during the first two years of the war were little more than extensions of traditional military formations and units. In August 1915, for example, the Royal Engineers created 11 labour battalions, which employed navvies – tradesmen and semi-skilled men – for the construction of rear lines of defence and other works.[10] Attempts to address frontline labour requirements were also made by creating 12 infantry labour battalions within infantry divisions. These pioneer battalions were trained as infantry but were normally engaged in labour and were composed of men who had mining and road-laying experience, or who had other usable trades or skills.[11] Further labour was created following the passage of the Military Service Act of March 1916 by the establishment of a non-combatant corps of eight companies comprising conscientious objectors.[12]

Non-European military labour

Except for the active involvement of the Indian Army in France during the first year of the war, when Britain's decimated professional army fought desperately to stem the German advance, British policy ruled the Empire's black and coloured subjects out of frontline, combatant service in Europe.[13] This aversion to allowing black and coloured men to bear arms against white men was evident on the Western Front throughout the First World War, 'but not elsewhere in the Middle East or Africa, where the major opponents could be characterised as themselves coloured'.[14]

The use of coloured military units as labour on the Western Front was, however, something that it was less difficult to reconcile, and in July 1916, for example, it was decided 'to bring two battalions of the British West Indies Unit from Egypt to France (Fig 2.2), and to recruit the Cape Coloured Labour Battalion'.[15] These units became labourers behind the

Fig 2.2 Members of the British West Indies Regiment on the Somme, 1916. [© Imperial War Museum Q1202]

7

lines in France, 'building roads and trenches, unloading and transporting munitions and other stores, and performing a host of other indispensable but seldom acknowledged jobs'.[16]

Although a military contribution from them was not viewed with favour, the Empire's coloured populations did present a possible solution to Britain's acute, ongoing military labour shortage, and the idea of recruiting civilian coloured labour was mooted as early as March 1916, when the War Office suggested bringing Egyptian labourers to France. A few months later, the War Office proposed recruiting unemployed Chinese dockers from within the UK to work in France, and in the autumn of that year decided to bring an Indian labour corps to France, although the first contingent of the latter did not arrive until April 1917.[17]

By the end of October 1916, the unskilled labour force on the Western Front totalled 800 officers and 78,000 other ranks.[18] Two years later, at the end of the war, this labour apparatus had swollen to 389,900 men, 11 per cent of the total strength of the British Army.[19]

The wartime labour force, comprising mainly civilian contract labourers from, principally, South Africa, Egypt, India and China, was the foundation of Britain's logistical support for its armies, and 'although precise numbers are hard to determine, the various coloured labour units appeared to have ultimately accounted for half the workers on the Western Front'.[20] According to Starling and Lee, this labour force consisted of 11 Royal Engineer battalions, 30 infantry labour battalions, 29 ASC companies, two ASC naval companies, two British West Indian regiment battalions, the Cape Coloured Labour Battalion, the Bermuda Royal Garrison Artillery, two South African Native Labour Corps battalions, eight non-combatant corps companies and 47 prisoner-of-war companies.[21]

The Directorate of Labour and the British Labour Corps

To simplify the complicated arrangements that resulted from the ad hoc genesis of the early labour contingents, the War Office decided, in 1916, to combine all British wartime labour in a general pool to supply all services. This labour pool became known as the British Labour Corps (BLC).[22] A body to manage this gigantic labour apparatus, the Directorate of Labour, was established under the command of Lieutenant Colonel Evan Gibb on 26 November 1916, and from January 1917 reorganised and streamlined the labour-corps system, drawing the many disparate units into a more coherent structure, under the badge of the ASC.[23]

The immediate issues faced by the Directorate of Labour, while trying to bring order to the system, were the need to keep the wheels turning, the huge increase in the number of labourers, great variance in the size of units and 'officers and men often unfit for the task in hand'. On top of this, massive amounts of labour were required to support three major offensives on the Western Front in 1917: Arras in April, Flanders between July and November and Cambrai in November.[24]

As a measure of the level of labour support that the British Army required, Gleeson comments that 'to maintain a single army division [between 10,000 and 20,000 men] for one day, nearly 200 tons of deadweight supplies and stores were required'. In 1914, the army consisted of six divisions. By the end of the war it had ballooned to 60.[25] To keep pace with the demand, labour sourced in Britain increased from 82,000 to 145,000 men in 1917, the number of prisoners of war set to labour rose from 20,000 to 70,000 and coloured labour grew a staggering 50-fold, from roughly 2,800 men to 145,000.[26]

Labour units ranged from 2,000-strong South African Native Labour Corps battalions to small, 100-strong non-combatant corps companies. The larger battalions, over 1,000 strong, created a headache for the Directorate of Labour, being too big for labour purposes. To be effective, these large units had to be split into smaller detachments, 'which were often scattered over a wide area, to the detriment of both discipline and organization'. The original 500-strong ASC companies had proved to be a convenient size and it was decided that all other labour units would also be organised in companies of 500, all ranks, consisting of four platoons.[27] While this solved some problems, it caused others.

Starling and Lee observe, for example, that Army regulations meant the officer commanding a labour company had the authority to exercise the full powers of punishment laid down in paragraph 493 of the King's Regulations. An officer could deal with such punishments summarily, without reference to anyone else, could dock pay and could administer field punishments. Many of the men who found themselves in charge of the resized labour companies, especially those arriving with coloured or foreign labour units, were inexperienced in command and in dealing with disciplinary matters. This inevitably led to tensions and abuses in many units, which will be touched on in Chapter 11.[28]

The Foreign Labour Corps

Despite the size of the BLC, by early 1917 it was clear to the War Office that the unprecedented scale of the conflict and toll in men, on the Western Front in particular, and the amount of labour required to ameliorate the burden of labour fatigues on frontline infantry could not be met from within the United Kingdom. The decision was therefore taken to recruit foreign labour on fixed-term contracts from British overseas territories and beyond. In the last two years of the war, roughly 300,000 foreign labourers were engaged, of whom 195,000 served on the Western Front. These foreign labourers were additional to those in the BLC recruited from Britain, so that by the end of the war, Britain had an active labour force, in units of various sorts and across all fronts, that numbered close to 700,000 men.

Indian labour units had been working in France and Belgium since 1915, but as a result of the new recruitment policy, labour contingents soon began arriving from Africa, the Middle East, Asia and the Caribbean. These labour corps were employed outside the UK in almost all circumstances, due to trade union pressure not to allow foreign labour into Britain.[29]

Although this foreign labour did ease the burden on British labour units, its rapid influx also brought with it other problems for the Labour Directorate. Housing and feeding these large numbers of recruits was a challenge in itself. Added to this were the restrictions placed on coloured labour by both Britain and some of the home countries like South Africa. For example, black SANLC members were not allowed to leave their camps unless accompanied by a European officer, while Chinese Labour Corps members were not allowed to mix with the Chinese employed by the French. Tribal differences within the Indian Labour Corps (ILC) meant that great care had to be taken with the composition of individual ILC companies.[30]

The fact that the various foreign labour corps were civilians on contract, rather than enlisted or conscripted military personnel, added the issue of contracts, particularly their conditions and duration, into an already complex situation. Units like the Cape Coloured Labour Battalion, the BWIR and the Fijian Labour Corps were all employed for the duration of the war. The various foreign civilian corps, however, were on different contracts: the Egyptian Labour Corps members were contracted for six or seven months (dependent on where they were deployed), SANLC and Indian Labour Corps contracts were for a year, and the Chinese had signed up for three or five years.

Problems arose around the interpretation of whether contracts ran from the individual time of recruitment, from embarkation for France or from when labourers arrived in France. Confusion around this issue caused substantial unhappiness, and delays in repatriating men after the expiry of their contracts, in part due to a shortage of ships, exacerbated the situation and resulted in unrest and even mutiny within a number of the labour corps in late 1917 and 1918.[31]

The rest of this chapter provides a brief introduction to Britain's First World War foreign labour contingents on the Western Front and touches on those deployed in the other theatres of war. More detailed discussion of the South African Native Labour Corps and Chinese and Egyptian Labour

Corps, which expands on some of the common areas of experience of foreign labour in France, is provided in Chapter 11.

The Chinese Labour Corps

In late 1916, China was neither part of the British Empire nor was it yet a belligerent in the global conflict. In August 1914, the British minister in China had rejected an offer from the Chinese president of 50,000 troops for a campaign to reclaim Tsingtau[32] from German control.[33] Keen to forge links with the Allies, however, the Chinese Government then offered to provide labour instead, which was something both Britain and France soon came to appreciate the potential benefits of.[34]

The French Ministry of War first considered the possible use of Chinese labour in France as early as March 1915, but opposition from senior members of the military saw the idea shelved for a number of months. By June of that year, however, the idea began to gain traction, and in November 1915 the Ministry decided to go ahead with the proposal.[35]

As China was a neutral power until 14 August 1917, when it declared war on Germany, the initial recruitment of Chinese nationals by France and then Britain had to be delicately handled. Both countries were able to circumvent the neutrality issue by recruiting the Chinese as non-combatant labourers and by having their employment contracts negotiated privately, although with the knowledge of the Chinese Government. In the case of France, the Chinese set up the Huimin Company in May 1916, a private company that France then contracted to recruit labourers.[36] A confidential letter to the War Office from the British military attaché in Peking (now Beijing), dated 3 October 1916, contains a précis of the French contract and conditions, and it seems that the British later recruited their Chinese labourers on a similar basis.[37]

The recruitment of Chinese labour by both Britain and France was thus contrived as a private, commercial and civilian undertaking, with a syndicate of Chinese businessmen agreeing to supply the labourers, 'in order to avoid neutrality questions'.[38] In contrast, the recruitment of the other foreign labour contingents from various British territories and dominions across the globe was a more political and politicised issue, referencing as it did the complex relationships of the countries involved, and those recruited, with Imperial Britain.

Regarding the legal position of the Chinese labourers prior to China's entry into the war, Fawcett remarks that the basis on which they were employed meant that they were viewed as mercenaries. What effect this may have had on official and military attitudes to them is something that seems not yet to have been explored.[39]

Like France, Britain was initially reluctant to accept the offer of Chinese labour. This stemmed from political concerns about China's position in world geopolitics and its real intentions in offering the Allies help. There was opposition within the UK by organised labour and racial considerations, of the sort that was also voiced in South Africa the same year when the formation of the SANLC was proposed.[40] As the crisis around labour deepened in 1916, however, the British authorities were compelled to re-evaluate their stance and by July of that year the Army Council had decided to recruit Chinese labourers to work in France.[41] The French Government was notified of this intention and gave its approval, as long as the labourers were subject to military law.[42] British recruiting began, and the first contingent of 1,078 labourers left Weihaiwei,[43] a port on the Yellow Sea leased by Britain, in January 1917, arriving in France via Canada on 19 April (Fig 2.3).[44]

Fig 2.3 Chinese Labour Corps recruiting in Weihaiwei. [© South China Morning Post]

Despite the legal smoke and mirrors, once Germany discovered what Britain and France were doing there were fierce protests from the German Embassy in Peking to the Chinese Government. The Chinese authorities responded by pointing out that the workers being recruited went to Europe in a private capacity and had been recruited by private companies. China could thus not be accused of compromising its neutrality.[45]

By late 1917, Britain had a Chinese Labour Corps (CLC) in France of 50,000 men, and by the end of the war, that number had increased to 96,000. The French employed 30,000.[46] The Chinese were to remain in

France for far longer than any of the other foreign labour corps. Many recruits returned to China only in 1921, having been engaged in salvage, battlefield clearance and reconstruction work following the end of the war.[47]

The conditions under which the Chinese were housed and managed were far less stringent than those required by the South African Government for its black labourers. The corps was housed in compounds only in the rear areas and managed its own catering and camp discipline, without the need for British guards.[48] The apparent stability of the CLC, in comparison with the other foreign labour corps, which were disbanded both before and immediately after the cessation of hostilities for reasons that will be discussed later (*see* Chapters 11 and 12), is perhaps linked to their non-partisan position. They were not British subjects and thus had no political agenda to their participation in the war. Their enlistment was a commercial transaction that was not bound up in the sort of political issues that were a feature of the other foreign labour corps.

The Egyptian Labour Corps

Another major influx of foreign contract labourers into France was the Egyptian Labour Corps (ELC), the first contingent of which arrived in March 1917. The corps was created because the army needed labour at Gallipoli, and grew from an initial 3,000 men to anywhere between 250,000 and possibly more than one million men. Poor recordkeeping and the re-enrolment of many men after their initial period of recruitment account for these wildly divergent figures.[49]

The vast majority of Egyptians served in the Middle Eastern campaigns, principally in Greece and Mesopotamia, but 18 companies were deployed to ports in France and Italy.[50] Beyond these basic statistics, there is very little other information available about the ELC, particularly the contingent that went to France.

One thing that is clear about the ELC is that the recruiting methods applied were robust. A number of authors refer to it as a new form of *corvée* – the unpaid labour obligations exacted by a feudal lord – and suggest that it amounted to 'compulsory volunteering'.[51] Violence was a characteristic of the recruitment campaign, with officials meeting their quotas by any means necessary.[52] One of the official figures given for Egyptians recruited for military labour service during the war is 327,000. Hacker suggests that 75 per cent of this total may have been forced labour. This forced labour seriously disrupted local economies and has been pointed to as a key factor in the large-scale Egyptian peasant revolt of 1919.[53] An alternative view of labour recruitment in Egypt is that it was only slightly resisted and that many *fellahin*[54] sought such employment because it paid relatively well.[55]

The first request for Egyptian labourers to be sent to France was received by the War Office in January 1917. A thousand labourers were requested as stevedores in southern French seaports, particularly Marseilles, with a further 10,000 needed on the Western Front the following month (Fig 2.4).[56]

Fig 2.4 Men of the Egyption Labour Corps handling stores at the quay, Boulogne, 12 August 1917. [© Imperial War Museum Q2703]

The labourers were contracted for relatively short periods – six months on the Western Front and seven months in Marseilles. As with the SANLC, there were restrictions on their movements, and when not employed, ELC members were required to stay in camp. The officers and the non-commissioned officers of the corps were found to be largely unsuited for the job they were hired to do. Very few of the officers could speak any Arabic, and as a group they had almost no military experience.[57]

The shortness of the Egyptian labour contracts – which were measured in terms of time in France – required a high and steady rotation of units, and disputes over the termination of contracts and repatriation led to several strikes, at least two of which turned violent.[58]

Other foreign labour contingents

Other foreign labour contingents in France came from all over the world. In addition to the 21,000-strong Indian corps, smaller numbers of labourers were recruited from Bermuda, the West Indies, the Seychelles, Mauritius, Fiji, North and West Africa and Madagascar and employed by the British in France and Flanders.

The SANLC is discussed in detail in the subsequent chapters but it was not the only South African labour on the Western Front. In September 1916, the 2,000-man Cape Coloured Labour Battalion arrived from South Africa. Widely known as the 'Cape Boys', with white officers commanding coloured labourers, the unit mainly worked on the docks at French ports, where they were joined in 1917 by another South African coloured unit, the 4,200-man Cape Auxiliary Horse Transport.

South Africa drew a sharp distinction between coloureds and blacks; no blacks served with the Cape Boys or the Horse Transport and these units were not billeted in closed compounds as black South African labour units subsequently were. Both of these units remained in France after the armistice, doing general salvage work and horse demobilisation, and were repatriated only in July 1919.[59]

In other theatres of the war, foreign labour contingents employed by the British included, in addition to those already discussed, Russians, Serbs, Macedonians, Maltese, Kurds, Arabs, Persians (Iranians), Adeni from Yemen and a Jewish Labour Corps.[60] Where these corps were not local to the area, they were drafted in to supplement local labour when that proved inadequate to meet the demand.

Although many of these labour corps were active behind the lines – for example, on the Western Front – others were involved in the transport and delivery of supplies and ammunition directly to frontline positions, often under heavy enemy fire.[61]

The invisibility of the labour corps system

Although huge numbers of Britons and citizens of the Empire served in the labour system during the First World War, the entire system is largely invisible in the vast literature of the war. The labour corps system receives just four mentions in the official history of the war and is rarely mentioned in regimental histories. Although foreign labour contingents made a massive contribution to the British and Allied war effort, as a group they also remain largely invisible in the official histories and the bulk of secondary literature relating to the First World War.

There is an almost total absence of information about the native labour contingents used in the African theatres of war in the literature of the war, a phenomenon not limited to the South African labour corps. Despite the fact that the largest mass mobilisation of labour ever seen in Africa took place during the First World War, there is only a handful of articles and books that have examined the use of black labour, particularly in East Africa, during the conflict.[62]

Some sources suggest that the lack of published information on the labour corps system – both foreign and British – is partly because many of the records of this period were destroyed during the Second World War. It seems more likely, however, that the Labour Corps is simply a neglected area of First World War scholarship, which is symptomatic of a general neglect in literature of the non-combatant labour that serviced troops during the numerous major conflicts of the last two centuries.[63]

SANLC records

The administrative peculiarities of the SANLC – funded by Imperial Britain but administered by the Department of Native Affairs in the Union of South Africa, with its white officers falling under the ambit of the Union Defence Force – resulted in a complicated network of correspondence related to the corps. To compound matters, the records of the corps are fractured and much is missing. The Public Records Office in Kew in London had kept the Imperial records of First World War British foreign labour, including the SANLC, but was bombed during the Second World War and many of these records were lost.

In South Africa, according to the archivist at the South African National Defence Force Archives in Pretoria, there was a dispute after the First World War as to who should keep the SANLC records: the military turned them down because the SANLC was a scheme under the Department of Native Affairs, but Native Affairs viewed them as a military responsibility. Whatever the veracity of this story, what is clear is that much of the record of the SANLC has been destroyed or cannot currently be located. The possibility of the latter stems from the fact that the archive repositories in South Africa have large numbers of boxes of unsorted or undocumented records, some of which may contain material related to the SANLC.

The Cape Archives in Cape Town hosts some information from the Eastern Cape on the SANLC, and the records in the National Archives in Pretoria are clearly incomplete. The records in the South African Defence Force Archives include many of the attestation forms for the men of the SANLC. The racial policies of Government and the military at the time meant that the same attention to, and level of, detail captured in white service records was not required or recorded for black labour recruits. The attestation forms were, therefore, largely limited to a categorisation of the men according to their place of origin, their chief or headman, their names and some other very basic information. The limited literacy of most black recruits meant that they relied on translators or on the interpretation of white officials, who displayed varied levels of concern regarding accuracy in the information they recorded on the attestation forms.

The South African archives also reflect the biases of the time. For example, only positive letters written by members of the SANLC were retained in the records, reflecting the South African authorities' concern that the scheme be seen as successful. Beyond this there is little trace of the personal voices of the men of the SANLC, and the surviving archival material comprises the administrative records and recollections of white officials. Because the majority of black men in the SANLC were illiterate, there are few surviving written recollections of their experiences. The few that do exist were produced by men fortunate enough to have received a formal education and are not necessarily representative of the views of the vast majority of the men in the SANLC.[64]

3

South Africa and the outbreak of the First World War

When war broke out in August 1914, it was not only Britain that was at war, but also its dominions, those semi-independent polities that constituted the British Empire and included Australia, Canada, India, New Zealand and South Africa. Although the dominions enjoyed autonomy over the administration of their internal affairs, Britain retained control over their foreign affairs. As a result, when Britain was at war, so too were they, and with a combined population of roughly 400 million, they had the potential to provide Britain's war effort with an almost unlimited supply of people and materiel.[1]

The fledgling Union of South Africa was a recently created composite of the British Cape and Natal colonies and the former Boer South African (or Transvaal) Republic and Orange Free State under the Crown. The Union was a political result of the settlement reached between Britain and the mainly Afrikaans-speaking Boer republics at the Treaty of Vereeniging, which ended the South African War or Second Anglo-Boer War (1899–1902) in May 1902. Although the Treaty ended the war, and the Act of Union in 1910 gave back to the former Boer republics a measure of political independence, the South African War 'entrenched a bitterness between Boer and Briton which was to endure throughout the twentieth century'.[2]

British dominions could decide the extent of their involvement in any conflict and so, while South Africa bore a constitutional obligation to support Britain and could not remain neutral, it did have the latitude to decide on the nature and level of support it wished to give.[3] Although on the face of it South Africa's entry into the war was a fairly rapid and apparently easy one, the involvement of the Union in the war was strongly influenced by the prevailing political climate and the recent history of the country. With memories of the South African War still fresh and wounds still raw for many South Africans, the Union was a tangled mess of conflicting loyalties and divergent allegiances and was anything but united in its attitude to the new conflict.[4]

The Prime Minister, General Louis Botha, and his Minister of Defence, General Jan Smuts, were keen that South Africa participate, not only because it would fulfil the required imperial duty but also because they believed it would, in the long run, strengthen the cause of South African independence from Britain.[5] The decision to enter the war was voted through by the South African Parliament on 9 September 1914.[6] Botha informed Britain that the Union Government would accept responsibility for the defence of South Africa, thereby releasing British troops still on garrison duties in the country for overseas military service.[7]

The other dominions also contributed troops to support Britain, with Australians, New Zealanders, Canadians and Indians, among others, all fighting with distinction in the various theatres of the war, but particularly on the Western Front in France.[8]

Recruitment into South Africa's Union Defence Force (UDF) was on a voluntary basis, rather than conscription, and white and coloured volunteers were soon swelling its ranks. During the course of the war, UDF troops served in many theatres – initially in German South-West Africa and German East Africa, and then in the Middle East, in the Dardanelles and on the Western Front.

Afrikaner rebellion

Many Afrikaner Nationalists responded to South Africa's entry into the war by declaring themselves neutral and refused to support Britain, arguing that it placed at risk the peace and prosperity of the Union.[9] Others, however, believed more drastic steps were required, and a rebellion broke out, with roughly 11,472 mainly Afrikaans-speaking rebels taking to arms

An Unwelcome Visitor.

SOUTH AFRICAN UNION : Vile reptile, your head must come off at once!

The treachery of Colonel Maritz in command of British troops in the north-west of the Cape Province, South Africa.

Thursday, October 15th, 1914.

Fig 3.1 The Afrikaner Rebellion, cartoon from The Mail, *15 October 1914. [Courtesy of Cartooning the First World War, Cardiff University]*

in an attempt to topple the Government. South Africa's entry into the war was the catalyst for the uprising, but its underlying causes ran much deeper: a general dissatisfaction with the Botha Government, a desire to re-establish independent Boer republics lost during the South African War, and the hopes held by many poor whites of greater wealth and security (Fig 3.1).[10] The rebellion was swiftly suppressed, but it delayed the start of the South-West African campaign and divided the nation at a critical time.[11]

German South-West Africa and East Africa

South Africa's active entry into the war came in early September 1914 after Britain asked whether the Union would be willing to invade German South-West Africa (now Namibia) to seize the territory's important harbours and wireless stations.[12]

The Government agreed, albeit reluctantly, and more than 60,000 troops were mobilised for the campaign, massing on the border between the two countries, under the command of General Henry Lukin and Lieutenant Colonel Manie Maritz. A third force was dispatched by sea to occupy the port of Lüderitz. Within a little more than nine months, German South-West Africa had fallen to the South African forces, which were then deployed to the long, arduous and ultimately inconclusive campaign against the elusive General von Lettow-Vorbeck in German East Africa (now Burundi, Rwanda and the mainland portion of Tanzania).[13]

The labour contingents supplied by South Africa for both of these campaigns will be discussed in the following chapter.

Black South Africans and the outbreak of war

For black South Africans, the period between the 1902 Treaty of Vereeniging and the outbreak of the First World War in August 1914 was marked by a series of political setbacks that were to have a distinct bearing on their reaction to and experience of the war.

The 1902 peace treaty set in motion the processes that resulted in the political unification of the British Cape and Natal colonies and the Boer republics of the Transvaal and Orange Free State in 1910. The 1910 Act of Union was the foundation of a modern, industrial and self-governing South African state.

At the end of the South African War there was an expectation among black South Africans that the British victory promised a better future for them. This was not to be. The terms of the Peace of Vereeniging and 'the calculated indifference of the subsequent British administration' to the political, economic and social aspirations of South Africa's black majority were a bitter disappointment, particularly since large numbers of black South Africans had served the British side during the war, as both combatants and non-combatants.[14]

The 1910 constitution of the Union of South Africa dealt another blow to black political aspirations. It denied the franchise to all but a minority of black South Africans in the former Cape Colony, which had historically enjoyed a limited franchise, and thereby perpetuated the exclusion of the vast majority of South Africans from the formal political process.[15]

After Union, the system of passes developed in the late 19th century as the mining industry grew was systematically enforced to restrict and control the movements of South Africa's black population.[16] And then, in 1913, the Natives Land Act dealt a further major blow by removing the right of black South Africans to own or lease land except in designated reserves, which made up only 7.3 per cent of the total area of the Union. The legislation was the culmination of a process that had been under way for at least 100 years in South Africa and was designed to destroy a thriving, independent or semi-independent rural black peasantry by forcing it off the land. The landless black majority was concentrated into small pockets of poor land, which could not possibly support the population and which became pools of wage labourers to supply South Africa's mines and burgeoning heavy industry.[17]

The years immediately prior to the First World War were thus a time of increasing black political ferment and struggle. The political setbacks of the previous decade served to unify black political activity and, in 1912, several hundred of South Africa's educated black elite formed the South African Native National Congress (SANNC) – which would be renamed the African National Congress in 1923 – to protest against racial discrimination and to appeal for equal treatment for blacks under the law. The educated elite who formed the backbone of the SANNC maintained a belief that Britain would not completely abandon black interests in South Africa (Fig 3.2). For them, 'colonial modernity was not without its paradoxes ... Having styled themselves as modernists, [they] were ... left out of the promises of the very same ideas and social formations that they had invested themselves in'.[18]

Black responses to the declaration of war were varied. Some, particularly the educated elite, saw the war as an opportunity to prove their loyalty in the hopes of furthering their cause for more political rights.[19]

At the outbreak of hostilities in August 1914, the SANNC therefore adopted a loyalist stance in their reaction to South Africa's entry into the war. Its honorary President, Dr Walter Rubusana, conveyed to General Smuts a pledge by the Congress of loyalty to the cause.[20]

Fig 3.2 SANNC delegation to London in 1914. Left to right: Thomas Mapike, Revd Walter Rubusana, Revd John Dube, Saul Msane, and Sol Plaatjie. The delegation tried to get the British Government to intervene against the Natives Land Act. [https://xh.wikipedia.org/wiki/File:ANC1914.jpg]

The Executive of the [SANNC] desires to assure the Union government that this Congress is absolutely loyal to the Union of South Africa and to inform the government that during the present European crisis if any assistance or sacrifice is required by the government from us we shall be ready and willing to be on our places.

We fully realise that our lot is one with that of white South Africans. Moreover, in order to prove our loyalty to the government, the Executive has unanimously decided to suspend all agitation against the Natives Land Act until the present unrest is over.

Yours respectfully,
Dube, President,
Seme, Treasurer.[21]

The SANNC also offered to raise 5,000 black troops for service in the planned military campaign in German South West Africa.[22]

This cooperative stance by South Africa's main black political party was not, however, an indication of passive acceptance of a subservient position. It was motivated by political considerations. With virtually no avenue still available to black South Africans to bring about constitutional change, the SANNC leaders believed that if they identified themselves with the war effort they could expect to be rewarded for their loyalty with meaningful political recognition by both the white ruling class and the British Crown.[23]

For most black South Africans, however, the war was something distant and largely irrelevant: it was yet another 'white man's' conflict, far removed from South Africa and unlikely to impact on their lives, and certainly not positively.[24] The 1913 Land Act and its repercussions had convinced many not to support the Government in the conflict. Some men working on the mines even showed pro-German sentiments as Britain had clearly failed to champion their cause and Germany represented a new alternative.[25]

Government reaction

Fearful of the potential political consequences of arming the black majority, the SANNC offer of recruits was turned down by the South African Government, which nevertheless expressed its 'great appreciation of the loyal sentiments ... of the native citizens of the Union'.[26] According to the Government, 'the present war is one which has its origins among the White people of Europe and the Government are anxious to avoid the employment of its Native citizens in a war against Whites'.[27]

The Government had no desire to use people of non-European descent in a combative capacity in the conflict, despite the desperate need for more fighting troops. Its apparently magnanimous response was pure dissimulation and disguised the truth that the exclusion of blacks from the armed forces was a direct result of the racial fears and prejudices that permeated white South African society.

If blacks were allowed to join the UDF on a basis of equality in an armed capacity, most white South Africans believed that the existing nature of South Africa's racial relations would be threatened and 'the position of the white minority jeopardised by blacks trained in the use of firearms'.[28] Black men fighting alongside white troops against other 'European' races might incorrectly assume equality of rights and status, and in South Africa, this could disturb the political and economic status quo: a cheap, expendable, migrant labour force without any political power under white minority rule. There was a real fear that arming black men might lead to a full-scale black rebellion against the white minority.[29]

A secret Colonial Office report in 1915 by Bonar Law, the Secretary of Colonies, put this reaction into perspective, stating that 'no proposal for training Natives upon a large scale is likely to be acceptable to ... the British and Dutch inhabitants of the Union, as the return, after peace, of a large body of trained and disciplined men would create obvious difficulties and might seriously menace the supremacy of whites'.[30]

Furthermore, the establishment of the UDF in 1912 by the white ruling class in South Africa 'was in part an effort to ensure [its] continued dominance and control of the subordinated majority'. Although the Defence Act (13 of 1912) did not specifically exclude coloured, Indian or black South Africans from military service, only 'persons of European descent could be made liable to defend the country in time of war'. Article 7 of the Act limited the participation of persons of non-European descent to a non-combatant role, although this article could be repealed in a time of war.[31] The UDF was thus conceived not merely as a safeguard against external military threats but also as a force to be deployed in the event of black insurrection.[32]

Strangely, history shows that whites in South Africa had regularly and willingly accepted the use of blacks for military purposes – in the 18th- and 19th-century Frontier Wars in the Eastern Cape and during the South African War. Since they were most often deployed against other blacks regarded as threatening by the whites, however, their use was considered both necessary and tolerable.[33]

While black South Africans reacted indignantly to the Government's attitude, questioning why they should be excluded from participation in the war in which the blacks of other parts of the Empire were serving,[34] an opinion expressed in a white South African newspaper, the *East Rand Express*, on the proposal by the War Office to use Indian troops perhaps neatly captures the prevailing view of the white minority in South Africa with regard to the use of blacks as combatants:

> If the Indians are to be used against the Germans they will return to India disabused of the respect they should bear to the white race. The empire must uphold the principle that a coloured man must not raise his hand against a white man if there is to be any law and order in either India, Africa or any part of the Empire where the white man rules over a large concourse of coloured people.[35]

Rising pressure

Despite Bonar Law's appraisal of the sentiments prevailing in South Africa, the need for troops was such that, in 1916, the Colonial Office, at the behest of the War Office, made a tentative approach the South African Government regarding the possibility of raising an armed black corps for service in Europe.

Predictably, the Government's reaction was negative, and it made explicit in its response what had previously been understood but not stated: 'under no condition would the Government allow a black combatant force to proceed to Europe as this would endanger white South Africa'.[36]

That the Colonial and War Offices accepted this reply without demur is perhaps not surprising, and suggests that although the British war apparatus was desperate for troops, there were also strong reservations in important quarters in Britain that echoed South African concerns that:

> There would be no more peace for South Africa if it were to be put in the power of the natives to say to the Whites there: 'You tried to beat your White enemies in Europe without us, but you failed and had to call us in to finish the war'. The moral effect throughout the Union of sending native contingents to fight in the battlefields of Europe would be incalculably disastrous to the prestige of the Whites there.[37]

The British Government's acceptance of South Africa's refusal to consider black combat troops was clearly at odds with the SANNC's belief that they could be relied on to support black demands for political reform in South Africa. Black South Africans should perhaps have seen it as an omen of British Government responses to post-war events and representations.

Shift in position

Although unwilling to consider black combatant troops, Prime Minister Botha did want to further aid the war effort and, as pressure grew from Britain for South Africa to provide additional support, he realised that supplying labour would be one way of doing so. The South African Government was also afraid that unless it adopted a more helpful position, Britain might bypass its authority altogether and recruit men directly from Bechuanaland (now Botswana), Lesotho and Swaziland. These British protectorates, although not part of the Union of South Africa, nevertheless were an important part of the labour pool for South Africa's growing industrial sector, and therefore best kept under South African control. Botha decided that agreeing to the creation of a black military labour contingent would at least allow the Union to dictate the terms of service and keep South African officers in charge of the labourers, which would theoretically limit the labourers' exposure to unwanted foreign ideas and influences while deployed outside the borders of Southern Africa.[38]

Botha suspected that the decision to raise a South African black labour contingent for deployment in Europe would be met with opposition if it had to go through Parliament. The South African Government therefore specified that the raising of the black labour contingent would be an Imperial scheme, funded by Britain and facilitated by the Union. This allowed Botha to bypass Parliament altogether in the approval and creation of the SANLC.[39]

This ploy was successful and Botha was able to announce the start of recruiting of five battalions of black labourers for France in early September 1916. For many white South Africans, however, while there had been little interest in, or concern at, the active service of many thousands of blacks in the South West African and East African campaigns, their deployment in Europe was a completely different matter and a heated public debate continued in South Africa for many months after the announcement.

4

The birth of the SANLC: the African experiment

The obligation to do armed service in the UDF was limited to white South Africans, but blacks could be called upon to enrol as non-combatants. As South Africa embarked on two campaigns against German interests in Africa, the Government and public showed little squeamishness at using large numbers of black labourers to provide logistical support for white and coloured fighting troops.

The South African authorities seem to have believed that the use of blacks in an inferior military role as non-combatants in colonial territories within Africa was ideologically acceptable. The established black/white relationship remained undisturbed and 'there was little chance of South African blacks being exposed to significantly different ideological influences' that could later pose a threat to the white hegemony in South Africa.[1]

Solomon (Sol) Plaatje, a black court translator, author and newspaper editor, and General Secretary of the SANNC (*see* Fig 3.2), recognised with great insight at the time that 'it seems to have occurred to the authorities that the best course is to engage the Natives in a capacity in which their participation will demand no recognition'.[2]

German South-West Africa

The first deployments of black labourers in what was later to become the SANLC took place in German South-West Africa (GSWA) in January 1915, when the 40,000-strong UDF invasion force was supported by a large black labour contingent.

The biggest issue faced by the UDF in GSWA was not the German armed forces but the size of the territory and the nature of the terrain – for the most part desert or semi-desert. The campaign required the establishment and maintenance of extensive lines of communication and supply, and the challenge of supplying a fighting force dispersed across a vast territory necessitated an equally large logistical organisation. Within weeks of the start of the campaign, the Department of Defence in Pretoria was receiving daily telegraphs from the front exhorting it to launch into a full-scale recruiting drive for volunteer labourers.

A hastily prepared scheme to recruit thousands of uniformed workers for the GSWA campaign saw the birth of non-white military service in the UDF. During the six months of the campaign, approximately 33,500 non-white volunteers served in GSWA, drawn from across the Union, although the majority (28,000) came from the Eastern Cape and the former Transvaal province.[3]

Under the scheme, these volunteer labourers were contracted on behalf of both the Department of Defence and the South African Railways, for a period of four to six months. Remuneration was £3 per month, which included rations and a basic clothing issue of riding breeches or trousers, a jersey, a cap and a pair of boots and putties.[4]

The labourers were allocated to transport duty as drivers and remount orderlies for thousands of animal-drawn supply wagons, carts and artillery wagons, as railway and road workers and as general labourers to move stores and ferry munitions. Their largest contribution was in the construction of a rail link between South Africa and GSWA, and the repair of railway lines within GSWA destroyed by the German forces as they retreated (Fig 4.1).[5]

Fig 4.1 Black labourers constructing a railway line near Arandis during the German South-West African campaign. [Transnet Heritage Library]

The view of the Government about their role was articulated at the time by Colonel S M Pritchard, Director of Native Labour, who stated that the labourers were utilised 'for that class of employment that was exclusively or ordinarily suited to Natives – such as Drivers, [Wagon] Leaders, and general labourers'.[6] They were seen, according to Gleeson, as 'a quasi-military corps of non-combatants and not as fully fledged soldiers of South Africa' – a view that was continued in those corps recruited for both the subsequent East African campaign and for service in France.[7]

Although limited to support roles under the Union Defence Act, the labourers recruited for the GSWA campaign were accorded a UDF identity. They were issued with a UDF armlet and a distinguishing letter badge on their jerseys that indicated their muster: 'T&R' for Transport and Remount for animal drivers, leaders and those assigned to remount depots; 'O' for Ordnance for those working at general supply depots; and 'A' for those working in the supply of artillery and other ammunition.[8]

There is little on record of how they experienced the war against the Germans. Unlike the later SANLC contingent in France, which was deployed behind the lines, the nature of much of the work of the labour contingent in GSWA meant that it was often directly exposed to the dangers of warfare. At the battle of Sandfontein in September 1914, for example, a number of black transport riders came under German fire and were captured. Grundlingh cites cases of the mistreatment by the Germans of black prisoners of war during the campaign, with at least some of those captured being tortured and mutilated.[9]

Fig 4.2 The Cape Field Artillery marches along Adderley Street in Cape Town upon their return from German South-West Africa, 1915. Note the members of the labour corps also marching in the right of the photo. [Getty Images 82463240]

The GSWA campaign was an unqualified success for the UDF and the South African Government, and the first successful Allied campaign of the First World War. There is virtually no mention of the presence or activities of the large black labour contingent in histories of the campaign, such as Collyer's official records,[10] although a photograph of black drivers parading through the streets of Cape Town with the Cape Field Artillery suggests that the contingent was not denied absolutely all recognition (Fig 4.2).

Despite a lack of adequate recognition, this force of black labourers played no small role in the success of the GSWA campaign, making a vital contribution to the maintenance of the long lines of communication and ensuring that the wagon and train wheels of the South African Expeditionary Force kept rolling.

East Africa

The GSWA campaign was followed for the UDF by a long and bitter expedition in German East Africa that turned into the longest campaign of the war, ending only two weeks after the Armistice in Europe.[11]

East Africa was very different from German South-West Africa but equally, if not more, extreme in terms of the conditions faced by those fighting and working there. The lack of infrastructure in the region and a hostile tropical and sub-tropical environment required a well-developed logistical system to support the fighting. As in GSWA, South African black labourers of the Native Labour Corps again played a vital role in this theatre of war, with more than 18,000 men serving as transport drivers, dock and railway workers and as porters in areas of the interior not accessible by vehicular transport.

The logistical planning for the conduct of this campaign was better than it had been in GSWA, and the military authorities – both British and South African – were able to give an early indication of their requirements. It was envisaged that approximately 12,000 black labourers from South Africa would be required for service in that theatre. Eventually, the Department of Native Affairs oversaw the recruitment and dispatch of more than 18,000 black South Africans to German East Africa between 1916 and 1918, with an average of 7,500 and 8,000 SANLC members always in the theatre.[12]

Once in-country, a Controller of Union Labour East Africa saw to the deployment of the men. About one-third of these labourers were deployed at ports or at supply depots on the railways, where they were used for unloading incoming supply ships and loading freight onto the railway for transport inland. Others worked in the interior, in transport, driving or leading animal-drawn vehicles, or in the remount group, which saw to the disembarkation of animals, their care at the depots and their transportation to bases in the interior. As in GSWA, some labourers were employed to construct new railway lines and to maintain and repair those already built by the Germans in their East African colonies. Although some of the corps was stationed at main centres and intermediate depots almost permanently, artillery drivers and porters, for example, were almost continuously on the move and shared the hardships of the troops in the field, subject to hunger and disease, and frequently coming within range of action on the front line.[13]

During the initial stages of the campaign, the black labour contingent was virtually indispensable, particularly in respect of the handling and driving of animals, and their work on the railways was praised by the British authorities for being quick and efficient. As the campaign dragged on, however, with the British and South African forces being led a dance across the region by the wily German commander General Paul von Lettow-Vorbeck, so the South Africans were drawn into the interior and then the unsanitary low-lying southern portions of German East Africa, where their health rapidly deteriorated.[14]

On paper, at least, there were medical services and hospitals sufficient to meet the needs of the South African troops and labourers. Similarly, the labour corps diet of bread, *mielie* (maize) meal, meat and vegetables was, according to the medical authorities, suitable for the work and conditions they would experience.[15]

Neither the white South African troops nor the black labourers adapted over the long term to the rigours of the conditions and climate in East Africa. But whereas the fighting troops were able to rest up when they were immobilised by torrential rain, the transport labourers and bearers were constantly busy, the need to keep supplies moving not being subject to the vagaries of the weather. Their work was arduous and was made even more so by a horrifying array of tropical diseases and parasites, which took a particularly heavy toll on the black labour force.[16]

By the beginning of 1917, the number of men in the labour units who were unfit for daily duty had risen to almost 40 per cent of the draft, and the mortality rate was running above 30 per cent. These figures doubled by the end of March of that year.[17] Grundlingh provides detail, for early 1917, for a section of the corps that was quartered along the coast in a malaria-infested area: 1,600 of the 2,000 men (80 per cent) succumbed to diseases like malaria, dysentery and pneumonia, and the health of those who survived was often poor for the remainder of their lives.[18]

By April 1917, these sickness and mortality rates were causing concern in South Africa, not only among liberal politicians such as John Xavier Merriman but also within the Government in the person of Prime Minister Botha. While he declared that 'decent rationing, medical and hospital treatment for stricken African labourers ought to be a dictate of humanity', he was forced to conclude that 'however bad malaria may be in East Africa, [he was] unable to believe that the death rate [among the black labourers] … can be so much higher than among the European and coloured troops, unless there is much that is lamentably lacking in the military arrangements for rationing and medical and hospital treatment'.[19]

This was the point at which the South African Government ceased recruiting labourers for the East African campaign, despite protests from the military authorities there. How much the decision to terminate recruitment was motivated by humanitarian concerns around the health and welfare of those recruited is impossible to accurately gauge, although Botha seems to have been genuinely concerned at the plight of the black labourers.[20] The motivation to end recruiting could have been driven just as easily by other considerations, one of which was the need to speed up recruiting for the labour contingent deployed in France.

African labour during the First World War

Black South Africans were not the only black Africans to be drawn into the war in Africa. Vast numbers of black Africans were enlisted or coerced into service in Africa in what became the largest mobilisation of labour ever seen in Africa, often under appalling conditions and with little regard for their welfare.[21]

Black African combat regiments were also raised for the campaigns in Africa and on other fronts. This included the Nigerian troops carried by the *Mendi* from West Africa to Dar es Salaam on the East African coast on the first leg of her last voyage (Fig 4.3).

The campaign in East Africa used more native workers than any other theatre of the war. Starling and Lee cite official figures of 66,580 coloured labourers employed in East Africa at the cessation of hostilities there on 23 November 1918.[22] However, the total number of natives employed between 1914 and 1918 probably exceeded one million. Killingray suggests that more than 810,000 of these recruits worked as carriers, and refers to the inscription on the Nairobi war memorial, which describes them as 'the feet and hands of the army'. Despite this, and possibly because the vast majority of these black Africans were not literate, there is less recorded about the work of the natives of Africa during the First World War than any of the other foreign labour units.[23]

As was the case in GSWA, and would be the case for the black members of the SANLC who subsequently went to Europe, the common experience of the South African black labour contingents was that while the whites involved in both the African campaigns were lauded for their efforts, there was no similar praise for the black labourers. Whether official or

Fig 4.3 Nigerian troops aboard the Mendi. *[© Imperial War Museum Q015435]*

not, the South African Government's de facto policy seems to have been to withhold any official acknowledgement that black South Africans were playing a role in the global conflict, as this might raise the sort of expectations that the SANNC was keen to see accrue to them through their participation.

Plaatje summed the situation up with his usual clarity: 'lest their behaviour merit recognition, their deeds and acts must, on account of their colour, not be recorded'.[24] Grundlingh expresses it similarly: 'the work force was taken for granted unless it caused problems; if it performed satisfactorily it could be ignored'.[25]

5

Native labour for France

The idea of sending South African black labour to France is credited to Josiah Wedgewood, British Member of Parliament and scion of the Wedgewood pottery dynasty. In 1915, Wedgewood was attached to the staff of General Smuts in East Africa and was so impressed with the work of the South African black labour contingent that he suggested to the Imperial War Council they consider the use of such labourers on the Western Front.[1]

The South African Government was, however, decidedly reluctant to entertain the proposal. Service by black South Africans in the African theatres of war like German South-West Africa and East Africa was something qualitatively different to their deployment in a European country. There was strong political and public opposition in South Africa to initial requests by the British authorities for such a labour contingent, with the opposition National and Unionist Parties voicing their opposition and even members of Botha's ruling South African Party objecting to the proposal.[2]

The core of these objections was the white belief that service overseas would raise black political consciousness and upset the delicate balance of power that allowed a white minority to dominate and control the black majority in South Africa. This was expressed by arguing that the scheme might result in blacks being 'socially and morally contaminated' in France. The need for wartime labour was recognised, but the consensus was that 'to send blacks to a European country in the turmoil of war meant that [they] might be exposed to less inhibited contact between blacks and whites'. This was therefore an undertaking that for white South Africans posed a considerable threat to the existing ideological order.[3]

There appears to have been a similar lack of enthusiasm in Britain for the recruitment of black Africans to alleviate the wartime labour shortage. The suggestion that black South African labourers could be employed within Britain 'was given short shrift [and] objections were raised on the grounds of race, discipline, efficiency and housing. In addition, British trade unions were implacably opposed to the possible displacement of their members by foreign workers'.[4]

The South African Government appears to have been less reluctant to dispatch coloured labourers to Europe than they were to consider the same proposal for black labour. This is demonstrated by the fact that on 11 April 1916, Lord Buxton, the Governor-General of the Union of South Africa, sent a telegram to the Secretary of State for the Colonies, reporting that the Government was willing to consider sending a contingent of coloured 'Cape Boys' for service in special labour battalions in France.[5]

Pressure and capitulation

The call for more labour from the War Office remained and grew increasingly strident with every passing month. Under intense pressure, the Colonial Office agreed to again broach the subject of a black labour contingent for deployment in France with South Africa, after obtaining the approval of the French Government.[6] One senior Colonial Office official regarded the whole thing 'as an experiment and a very doubtful and hazardous one' and 'considered it a pity that we could not have managed without employing them [black Africans] in Europe'.[7] Despite its initial reluctance, the South African Government, faced with sustained pressure from the War and Colonial Offices, finally capitulated and agreed to the creation and deployment of the SANLC in France. On 12 June 1916, the General Officer Commanding Cape Town was able to inform General Head Quarters in the UK that South Africa was prepared to provide 'labour battalions of Kaffirs for service in France', which would be known as the South African Native Labour Corps.[8]

Of all the black African subjects of the British Empire at that time, it was only those from South Africa – plus a small number of men from the neighbouring protectorates of Basutoland (Lesotho), Bechuanaland (Botswana) and Swaziland who joined the SANLC – who rendered war service in Europe.[9]

Government agreement and conditions

The mechanics of how it was possible for the South African Government to perform its apparently paradoxical about-face and agree to a scheme about which there were such deep national reservations were based on two important facts. First, the financial cost of the SANLC would be borne by the British Government. Prime Minister Botha was thus able to agree to and establish the corps and then proceed with recruiting without reference to the South African Parliament, effectively bypassing the political opposition to the scheme that could have stopped it in its tracks.[10]

Second, South Africa set a number of conditions that it required the War Office to meet before it would agree to the establishment and deployment of the SANLC. These conditions were laid out by Colonel S M Pritchard, Director of Native Labour (Native Affairs Department) and Officer Commanding the SANLC, at a meeting in France in October 1916 to agree the terms of its deployment with the Imperial War Council. South Africa required that the members of the SANLC would be segregated from other labour and military units and housed within closed compounds; that the SANLC would be administered under military law by South African officers; and that it would be employed outside the war zone, where it was easier to maintain the required segregation.[11] It was agreed that the most suitable employment 'would be quarrying, road making and forestry' because the 'difficulties of segregation which would arise in towns would be reduced if the Natives were engaged in such work'.[12]

The closed-compound system was a product of the South African mining industry, originating on the diamond mines at Kimberley. Using the barracks of the De Beers convict station in Kimberley as a model, workers' accommodation on the mines after 1885 was built as closed-in and fenced-off compounds (Fig 5.1). Workers entered the compound at the beginning of their contract and remained within it until their contract ended. Food was sold at the compound store and access between the compounds and the mines was by enclosed subways. One historical argument for the introduction of the closed compounds is that they were a mechanism for reducing the theft of diamonds, and later gold, by isolating workers from the outside world for the duration of their contracted period. Turrell argues, however, that these compounds had a more complex

Fig 5.1 This photo shows a single closed compound at the Kimberley mine. It is the large square structure in the distance. [© Africana Library in Kimberley]

meaning than that. They gave the mining houses tight control of their largely migrant labour force, an absolute necessity in developing South Africa's underground mining industry, where massive capital investment and concentration dictated the need for a stable, reliable and predictable workforce.[13]

The conditions insisted upon by the South African authorities were an attempt to isolate and insulate members of the SANLC from the inevitable 'contamination' that South Africans widely believed would come from contact with 'the social conditions of Europe'.[14] These arguments are couched in a manner that suggests that the welfare of the black members of the corps was the primary concern. The truth is that white South Africans wanted to keep any blacks sent to France cocooned from possible outside influences that might make them question their subservient social, political and labour position at home. How these conditions were translated into reality in France, and how they also seem to have come to be applied to other foreign labour contingents, will be explored in Chapter 11.

Once the decision had been taken to allow the SANLC to be formed, some white South Africans (some missionaries, officials of the Native Affairs Department and 'others with an interest in the "native problem"') realised that the scheme 'provided an ideal opportunity for testing – in what would, it was hoped, be carefully controlled conditions – the practicability and effects of the implementation of certain segregatory devices of social control'.[15] There appears to have been a belief that the results of the exercise could be utilised in South Africa after the war, and it has been suggested that another reason for General Botha's apparent personal enthusiasm for the formation of the SANLC may have owed something to the potential future uses the scheme could be put to in South Africa.[16]

Recruiting

Having agreed to provide black labourers for deployment in France, the Government lost no time in embarking on a vigorous campaign to recruit the men it had undertaken to supply. The initial target was to raise five battalions of 2,000 men, each with about 60 white South African officers and non-commissioned officers (NCOs).

Recruiting for the labour contingent in East Africa ceased and, instead, from September 1916, appeals were directed at volunteers to serve in France. This recruitment drive was extremely energetic and was driven by the black press, mission churches, magistrates and native commissioners, and through special recruiting meetings.[17] Some of the latter were addressed by Prime Minister Botha and by the Governor-General,

Lord Buxton, a mark of the importance the authorities attached to the
success of this scheme. Further evidence of the importance of the SANLC
initiative can be seen in the personal message sent by the Prime Minister,
who was also the Minister of Native Affairs, to the districts from which
men were being sought:

> I desire to express my appreciation for the good work which the Natives
> throughout South Africa have performed by furnishing labour for the forces
> in South Africa, South West Africa, and in East Africa. The service which
> they have rendered has greatly assisted the prosecution of hostilities. You
> have often expressed your great desire to be allowed to assist overseas, and
> at the request of His Majesty the King's government, it has been arranged
> that a contingent of 10,000 labourers should proceed to Europe for service.
> The contingent will be a military unit under military discipline, employed on
> dock labour at French ports and not in the fighting line and will be housed
> in closed compounds.[18]

Members of the Westernised black elite, who banked on African loyalty
during the war being translated into improvements in political and civic
rights, also lent their support to the recruiting drive.[19] Leading members
of the SANNC, including Sol Plaatje and the President of the Congress,
John L Dube, became involved in the campaign, 'stressing not only loyalty
to the King, country and empire, but the educational benefits of service
overseas, with France providing "a university of experience" for men to
work their way up the ladders of self improvement'.[20] To a large extent,
the support of the black elite can be best viewed as politically motivated,
but a considerable number of well-educated men actually enlisted with
the contingent, supporting the idea through action and not just rhetoric.
The belief in wartime service in the SANLC being translated into later
political reward is clearly evident in two documents written by recruits and
preserved in the Cape Archives:

> We are a people who are apt to learn if we are taught and we wish to be
> brought up in parliament ... that we should be trained in the art of carrying
> weapons that we may 'do our bit' when the war breaks out again. We are
> British subjects and we must share the fate of the Empire and we don't wish
> to be treated like women. We would like to be made the army of His Majesty
> with which he can crush his enemies.[21]

> When a native has shown his loyalty and good behaviour during the big war
> I hope the members will realise that this is not the first time for our chiefs
> and people to show themselves loyal to Government. ... Let the Government

today think of a Native, let the Empire know that the Natives of South Africa should be given the situation of better rights.[22]

Educated Africans – clergymen, teachers, translators, clerks, businessmen and other black professionals – enlisted in the corps in numbers quite disproportionate to the tiny size of their class.[23] They included men like the Reverend Isaac Wauchope Dyobha (of whom more later) and a flamboyant Ghanaian, a former newspaper editor rejoicing under the unusual name of Francis Zaccheus Santiago Peregrino, who published a pamphlet extolling the virtues of the SANLC in glowing terms.[24]

Members of various black royal houses also volunteered: Henry Bokleni and Dokoda Richard Ndamase from the Pondo royal houses; Chief Bota and a grandson of King Moshoeshoe from Basutoland; Chief Mamabola from the Transvaal; a nephew of King Cetshwayo and a grandson of King Dinuzulu from Zululand, in what is now KwaZulu-Natal, to name but a few.[25] Although some of these men probably genuinely supported the cause, others may have anticipated political and material benefits accruing from their support. For example, Chief Mangala of Umtata in the former Transkei (now renamed Mthatha and part of South Africa's Eastern Cape province) demanded that the colour bar be removed before they volunteered. Needless to say, his requests fell on deaf ears.[26] Others, according to A K Xabanisa, probably joined the corps because they were 'concerned about [future] repercussions of not supporting government'.[27]

The bulk of SANLC recruits, however, were poor, uneducated and usually from South Africa's rural areas. Many enlisted in desperation, and simply because the corps offered an opportunity to earn a living, as the reality of the Natives Land Act and South Africa's other discriminatory legislation and policy began to be increasingly felt by the black majority. This seems to have been particularly the case in the (former) Transvaal province, where a severe drought meant that the SANLC offered an alternative to possible starvation. As a result, this area of the country eventually provided the bulk of recruits for the SANLC.[28]

As has been mentioned already, the catchment for recruiting extended beyond the borders of the Union, and substantial numbers of SANLC members came from what are now Lesotho, Botswana and Swaziland. In fact, an article in the *Botswana Daily News* in 2002 commemorating the role of Batswana men in both world wars refers to the 5th Battalion of the SANLC – the battalion associated with the *Mendi* – as the 'Protectorates Battalion'.[29] Medal rolls for Swazi, Sotho and Batswana members of the SANLC examined at the National Archives in Kew show that more than 2,000 non-South Africans served in the corps, making up nearly 10 per cent of its final total strength of 21,000.[30]

The struggle to recruit volunteers

There is a good deal of evidence to suggest that recruiting the number of men required for the corps was not easy and that appeals to join the labour contingent swayed relatively few.[31]

Many potential recruits did not consider the military wage of £3 per month (only about 10 per cent higher than the average mining wage) sufficiently high to compensate for the potential dangers attached to military labour.[32] South African industry, such as the Chamber of Mines, and other mass employers of black labour did not help either. For them, the recruitment of labour for France meant shortages in South Africa and demands for higher wages, and there was active resistance on their part to the recruitment programme.[33]

For many black South Africans, the call to serve 'was simply unattractive'. The departure of many primary breadwinners for service in the SANLC had the effect of 'increasing the household burden on those left behind, particularly women, children and elderly dependants'. One potential recruit told a meeting in Pretoria that, 'our women curse and spit at us for risking our lives for a government that maltreats Africans'.[34]

Perhaps the most important factor in the reticence of black South Africans to enlist in the corps was the fact that recruiting was done by South African organs of state, agencies and individuals, towards whom many blacks bore a deep distrust and antipathy, the result of years of discrimination, which had alienated the black population from the Government.[35] This was particularly the case in Natal Province (now KwaZulu-Natal), from where no more than 1,500 men were recruited into the SANLC. Part of the reason for this poor response was that only 10 years earlier, the Government had ruthlessly suppressed the Bambatha uprising, a Zulu revolt against taxation, and 'some of the officials who had been active in putting down the rebellion were [now] involved' in recruiting for the SANLC.[36]

Minutes of a meeting of the Transvaal Native Council reflect other issues that affected recruitment. They objected to the closed compounds being proposed for France, calling them a prison system, to the low rate of pay and to the fact that there was no provision for separation allowances for wives and dependants.[37]

In many areas of the country, the response to the call for men was so poor that coercion became widespread in assembling recruits.[38] Local chiefs were pressured by recruiters and government officials to provide recruits from their communities and often threatened with the loss of stipends, or even their positions, if they failed to raise their quotas.[39]

Further up the chain, district magistrates were being pushed by the Government's Native Labour Bureau to drive recruitment. A telegram from the Native Labour Bureau to the District Magistrate of Tembu in the former Transkei, for example, ordered magistrates to 'punish/suspend headmen who, having been summoned by you to attend the meetings have failed to do so and hold an enquiry into reason for neglecting this duty. Headmen who are showing no zeal should be called in and reprimanded and any particularly bad cases should be reported'.[40]

Some magistrates took these orders to heart, and it is fair to conclude that a degree of coercion was used to counteract poor recruiting results. The Magistrate of Kentane wrote to the Magistrate of Tembu describing a meeting he had called for recruitment purposes. Of the 59 headmen summoned, only 38 arrived, but because of bad weather on the day of the meeting, he recommended 'wholesale suspensions not be resorted to as it would be difficult to establish gross negligence'. He did admit, however, that he was 'putting on screw by declining to give out lands' and suggested that the Government should suspend subsidies, which would 'tighten things up considerably and result in the younger men being hustled'.[41]

It is difficult to say to what degree such strategies were actually used, but the very presence of these exchanges in the documents associated with the recruitment for the SANLC suggests that an acceptance of coercion, as a legitimate recruiting aid, was definitely present.

The Government tried to encourage recruiting by urging SANLC officers in France to send back to South Africa reports from SANLC members telling of their experiences overseas, so that these might be published with the hope of encouraging others to volunteer.[42] A circular to magistrates dated July 1917 from the Director of Native Affairs requested that they supply him with 'suitable letters received from Native members of the Contingent in France which may come to your notice or that of your officers from time to time and which are likely to have a stimulating effect on recruiting. The number coming forward is still poor and it is considered that the publication of letters from their compatriots would have beneficial results'.[43]

This policy may explain why the letters found in the official archives are only ever positive of the SANLC and the conditions in France and why they cannot therefore be taken as representative of the general opinion of the men involved. Positive reports were essential for the Government, to prove the scheme was a success and to keep good standing in the public eye. Two such endorsements read:

We were trained at Rosebank where all arrangements were excellent. On the way from home we had a very good journey, only very few men were sea-sick. After remaining in Plymouth Harbour for two days we went straight to France where we were given camps, warm food, warm clothing, far better than we were in the habit of wearing, and had mattresses to sleep on. Our first work was to chop trees ... We next went to Havre where we worked in the docks. Work went on all day and night, each detachment had regular hours in which they worked, 9 at a stretch. They worked hard and by doing so gained credit ... At times sections were given holidays, those who wished to play cricket played cricket and those who wished to dance danced, and we were all very happy ... We have no doubt that the English will win. We saw tanks, which were being off-loaded, ammunition, shells as big as ourselves ... On our way to England and back again we were very well guarded from submarines. None of us were ever sent into the firing line, the only danger we experienced were the German aeroplanes none of which returned to Germany. None of us were killed in the raids.[44]

We have seen most wonderful things of the civilized Nations and which things are innumerable to explain in the form of a letter. One thing France is most beautiful looking country mostly in the summer everything looks green; and it is what they called it – Green France. We enjoy ourselves in very many indoor games in the Y.M.C.A shop selling all what could be required by the men – and there are also in it billiard tables, a little library with a lot of newspapers and books all good to refresh memory. The weather now is very hot just like it is in South Africa in summer, and we have frequent ordinary summer rains. We see people of different tribes or I should say nearly every tribe under the British flag, all assisting in this great war and we are, therefore, not sorry to see ourselves forming a part of them as British subjects.[45]

These men may have been selected for their willingness to attest to positive experiences overseas but it is difficult to establish how much of this willingness stemmed from a true belief in the SANLC programme and how much from the prestige of being selected for the job and from the extra payment with which they were rewarded.

The Government was clearly upset at the lukewarm response to the recruiting drive and astonishingly put it down to the ingratitude of black South Africans. Botha reportedly saw it as a failure to discharge an obligation, given 'all that the Imperial Government and Union Government had done for them in the past'.[46] Other officials ascribed it to concerns by potential volunteers that their property would be stolen or damaged while they were away, or blamed it on the timing of the recruitment, which disrupted the seasonal ploughing. Some were more forthright, attributing the lack of volunteers to the 'laziness of the natives' – a racial slur typical of the time.

Either way, the Government and its agents appear to have been genuinely or wilfully blind to the real reasons why recruitment was poor, and seem to have come to believe their own propaganda: that black South Africans were incapable of independence of thought in the conduct of their own lives.[47]

Organisation of the SANLC

The structure of the SANLC battalions was simple. There were four companies per battalion, each consisting of 500 men, with a captain or major in command. In addition, each battalion had four other white officers, a company sergeant major and about 25 white and 30 black non-commissioned officers. The NCOs were chosen by the commanding officer of each battalion at the SANLC depot in Cape Town. The Secretary of Native Affairs appointed all chaplains, clerks and hospital orderlies. Only the white members of the SANLC were issued with weapons.[48]

Volunteers were sent from their place of enlistment to the SANLC depot in Rosebank (Fig 5.2) in Cape Town, mostly by rail. The first intake of recruits arrived at the depot on 8 October 1916.[49] At the time of their enlistment, all volunteers had to be attested as medically fit by a doctor. Prior to the medical examination, any men too weak for the work that would be waiting for the SANLC were weeded out by a weight test, which required each volunteer to carry a hundred-pound load over a distance of 100 yards (roughly 45kg over 90m).[50]

Fig 5.2 Quartermaster's store at Rosebank depot. [© African Studies Library at the University of Cape Town]

The SANLC contract was for 12 months and started and ended in Cape Town. This meant that the actual working time of any corps member overseas was reduced by up to three months when a period of training and travel to and from France was factored in. This was viewed as one of the major drawbacks to the scheme, but the South African Government insisted that a longer contractual period would severely deter potential recruits.[51]

The SANLC rate of pay (£3 a month) was met with opposition by the white public because it seemed that the men of the corps were far more generously paid than their white combatant counterparts: infantrymen received one shilling a day. However, the Government was quick to point out that the SANLC pay was fixed and did not include extra benefits or allowances to wives and families.[52] For the men of the SANLC, any money they wanted to send to their dependants had to be arranged out of their pay in a monthly stop order. SANLC men were also not allowed to draw more than one-third of their pay while in France. The rest, minus optional dependant allotments, accrued at home, to be paid out on their return to South Africa.[53] This stipulation was believed to be in the best interests of the men as it enforced saving and counteracted what was seen as their 'natural' predilection for wasteful expenditure, particularly on alcohol and women.[54]

One of the requirements for agreeing to the formation of the SANLC by the South African Government was that the corps would be officered by, and work under the supervision of, South Africans. The Government argued that British officers did not understand 'that considerable moral deterioration resulted from the failure to obtain a full day's work' from the labourers.[55] The white officers and NCOs who accompanied the corps to France were selected, in the main, because they were officials from the Department of Native Affairs or managers of mining compounds. What was required were men either 'intimately involved in the implementation of the Union Government's race policies or who were well-versed in controlling the black labour force on the mines'.[56] Experience in 'handling natives' and the ability to speak their languages was the key. Military experience was not a prerequisite.[57]

The result was that many members of the corps later referred to the 'brutal and barbarous' treatment they received from white officers while in France.[58] The description of the attitudes of officers in the SANLC by Robert Keable, an Anglican priest who travelled to France as a chaplain to the corps, bears out the result of the Government's approach to officering the corps: 'We found ourselves ... up against white officers who disliked "educated natives" and who particularly disliked natives in clerical dress. Their whole attitude was an attempt to deny all privileges. Black was black, and a boy was a boy,[59] however dressed, educated or entitled.'[60]

6

The SANLC goes to France

When sufficient numbers of men had gathered at the Rosebank depot (now the University of Cape Town football fields), they took the train to Cape Town station, marched to the harbour and from there embarked on their journey to France, a roughly seven-week trip. The *Kimberley Advertiser* described, in flowery, paternalistic prose, one contingent of the corps passing through Cape Town, apparently on their way to the harbour:

It was a bright South African summer day, and the holiday maker from the North was represented in hundreds along Cape Town's thoroughfares, when from athwart the paved causeway rang in sharp crescendo, the sound of martial tread. But 'twas not the Khaki-clad warrior from Australia, nor our own in like array, that drummed the cobbled thoroughfare. These were swart of face, slouch-hatted, and clad in blue – a working party, 600 strong, a stalwart, happy party whose *vivre* [sic] belied the close of many marched miles and strenuous labour. 'Twas a sight to be long remembered as the swinging stride, impeded at the railway entrance, was checked to 'mark time' – there was no 'foot sore', 'leg-weariness' in the manner they struck the earth in perfect time, and one might gather that discipline *esprit-de-corps,* and pride in their service, animated these swarthy soldiers of the King.[1]

The first contingent of 889 men of the 1st Battalion left Cape Town on the *Kenilworth Castle* on 28 October 1916. After a four-day stop-over at Plymouth, they arrived at Le Havre on 20 November.[2] The second contingent, comprising the remainder of the 1st Battalion, sailed on the *Benguela*, arriving in France on 10 December.

The conditions they experienced aboard the *Benguela* caused Prime Minister Botha to address the following complaint to Governor General Buxton:

Private letters have been handed to me describing the voyage of the *Benguella* [sic] ... I am sure you will agree with me that nothing could be more disastrous to our prospects of securing the labour supply which the Army Council so urgently requires than the unfortunate experience of the batch of Natives conveyed on the *Benguella* [sic]. Of course no one expects on a troop-ship the comfort and convenience of a passenger service, but I cannot imagine any excuse that could be reasonably offered for the inadequacy and defectiveness of the sanitary, cooking and wireless arrangements. The account which had reached me is serious enough to justify me in asking that it should be brought to the notice of the responsible authorities who, I think, should at least been joined to take the strictest care that there is no recurrence of anything of the kind.[3]

Beyond the crowded conditions on board, which were to be expected on a troopship, the 'disgraceful latrines' aboard the *Benguela* were a major complaint: a '3/4 inch pipe had to flush water and the urinations of 500 men ... the natural result was a continuous overflow on the decks'.[4] For a 36-day voyage, such unsanitary conditions were understandably objectionable.

Of greater concern, however, was the ship's malfunctioning equipment, as Reverend Lennox's complaint details:

We had a long voyage ... It was an anxious time on board when the wireless failed to transmit, and we heard our escort calling and calling to us, but we could not reply. Then the bursting of the boiler tubes, after which we lay helpless for nine hours, a 'sitting shot for a submarine' ... No doubt there were reasons for rushing the Battalion off from Rosebank as was done, but a very serious responsibility was incurred in doing so. Consider, for example, the condition as regards the wireless ... there were submarines off Dakar, at Madeira and off Ushant at the time we were there. Had one of them spotted us, he could have pumped a shot into us and sent us to the bottom, and we were dumb.[5]

Despite the unsatisfactory conditions aboard the *Benguela,* Lennox was pleased to mention that 'the discipline of the natives ... was perfect'.

The question of differing treatment and standards for black servicemen, more generally, had already been raised. An example of such thinking is evidenced in a telegram from Senior Naval Officer Simonstown to the Admiralty in London with regard to vessels and arrangements for transporting the SANLC to Europe. The writer asks the question: 'May ships carry larger proportion of natives than troops: if so to what extent?' A heavy red pencil cross in the margin next to this question suggests that this was not to be the case. The fact that the question was asked, however, shows that there was a distinction made in the minds of some between the labour corps and regular troops.[6] Rather than being found ethically problematic by authorities, such a suggestion is more likely to have been countered by Botha's concern that poor treatment might discourage recruitment for the SANLC, the success of which was of great importance.

In respect of the SANLC, there was also the issue of racism, with one non-military passenger on the *Galway Castle* complaining that he was 'forced to herd with natives on deck'.[7]

The 3rd, 4th and half of the 5th SANLC Battalions had all arrived in France by the end of January 1917, and in total 42 companies were sent from South Africa to France between October 1916 and October 1917.[8]

SANLC camps in France

The earliest South African arrivals were sent to Eawy Forest, where they quickly learned forestry skills. They spent a number of months in the area before being replaced by prisoner-of-war companies in March 1917.[9] Other SANLC companies were stationed at camps across Northern France: Seine Inferieure, Vaudricourt, '6' Dump Albert, Aveluy near Albert, Fricourt, Montauban-de-Picardie, Meaulte, Mondicourt, Froissy, Arques, Bertrancourt, Rebreuve, Dannes (three camps), Zeneghen, Audruicq, Dieppe, Rouxmesnil and Abancourt (Fig 6.1).[10]

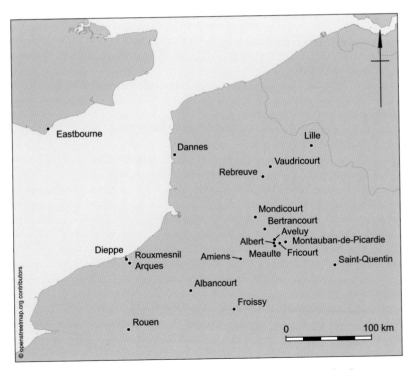

Fig 6.1 Location of SANLC camps, prior to March 1917. [© Wessex Archaeology]

From the outset, South Africa had been insistent that the SANLC must be based well behind the front line, partly because casualties might retard recruitment but principally because the cornerstone to the scheme, the complete segregation of the SANLC from other working and fighting units, was impossible to enforce in the army areas just behind the front.

The majority of the early SANLC camps listed above were, however, within the army areas, and conditions there meant that the corps could not be administered as rigorously as had been envisaged by South African officials. The establishment of the Labour Directorate at the end of 1916 diluted the power of South Africa over where battalions were to be placed. This is reflected in the deployment of the earlier SANLC companies to the camps near the front, where they were employed in a wide range of work – loading supplies, repairing roads and rail lines, lumbering in the forests of Normandy and quarrying stone[11] – not just the dock work at French Channel ports they had specifically and exclusively been recruited for.

Closed compounds and the tight security the South Africans demanded for the camps were at odds with the fluidity and movement associated with the area close to the front and it is possible that the camps provided were not as impervious as the South Africans would have wanted. The punishment book of one of the SANLC hospitals, discussed in more detail

Fig 6.2 SANLC with German prisoners of war, probably in Eawy Forest near Dieppe.
[© Imperial War Museum Q10238]

in Chapter 11, certainly suggests that men there were able to absent themselves from the camp without a great deal of difficulty.

The ever-increasing logistical pressures on the British Army's labour force in France inevitably led to the South Africans mixing in with other labour units, including prisoners of war (Fig 6.2). Indeed, there seems to be more evidence of the mixing of labour groups in the War Office records than the documents in the South African Official Record show.[12] These units were often not under South African command, and Colonel Pritchard, trying to maintain the official South African line about total control, bemoaned the more lax approach to managing the labour force this occasioned, suggesting it was 'bewildering and upsetting to coloured labour' and caused 'considerable moral deterioration'.[13] It is highly likely that the men of the SANLC thoroughly enjoyed the opportunity to mix with others and they probably found the experience stimulating and exciting rather than bewildering and upsetting.

Compounds and control

In spite of reality conspiring against the vision for the handling of the SANLC, the South African authorities in France tried their best to implement the system they had in mind and to sequester and cocoon the labour battalions from exposure to unwanted outside influences and ideas through the imposition of the closed-compound system.

According to specifications provided by the South African authorities, the compounds were to be large enough 'to contain all necessary buildings and a parade and recreation ground'. The men were housed in either wooden or Nissen huts,[14] each capable of accommodating between 12 and 30 individuals. Instead of the more usual wooden lining, the Nissen huts for the SANLC were given a felt lining, protected by wire netting, presumably to provide additional insulation for the South Africans, who were not accustomed to European winters.[15]

SANLC camps were to be surrounded by a six-foot-high fence, constructed of forest poles and with eight to ten strands of barbed wire. If the officer commanding any company felt it was necessary to provide more security or screening, sheets of corrugated iron were to be used. Wire netting or barbed wire could be strung along the top of the screen to prevent labourers climbing over. All openings in the fence were guarded, and access and egress was tightly controlled. The men were effectively imprisoned in their living quarters when they were not out at work.[16]

The layout of an SANLC camp is shown in a still image from a short propaganda film about the work of the corps in the Imperial War Museum's collection (Fig 6.3). The image clearly shows the wire fence

Fig 6.3 Unnamed SANLC camp in France. Screenshot from film in the Imperial War Museum.
[© Imperial War Museum IWM413]

around the camp, as do photographs of SANLC men carrying goods and fetching water at the camp at Dannes (Figs 6.4 and 6.5). The images also show wooden accommodation huts. Interestingly, in the photographs taken at Dannes, there appears to be a large marquee also erected within the camp.

Social control 'of a formidably intense kind' was the central tenet behind the SANLC compounds and in the minds of those in charge of the corps; it was as important to keep locals and non-SANLC members out of the camps as it was to keep the labourers in.[17] Every effort was made to prevent 'unauthorised persons from entering the camp[s] or conversing with Natives and especially to prevent all familiarity between Europeans and Natives, as this is subversive to discipline and calculated to impair their efficiency as working units'.[18]

Published notes distributed by the South African authorities to all officers of SANLC contained the following prohibitions, which were to be strictly enforced: black members of the corps were not permitted outside their camps, except when accompanied by an officer or white NCO. They were, furthermore, prohibited from entering any premises where liquor – wine, beer or spirits – was sold or being served. Keepers of cafés were forbidden to admit black South Africans or to serve them liquor. All houses and other camps were out of bounds to black labourers, and they were not allowed to enter shops or other business premises unless under

Fig 6.4 Fatigue party at the SANLC camp at Dannes, February 1917. [© Imperial War Museum Q7827]

Fig 6.5 SANLC party going to draw water at Dannes, February 1917. [© Imperial War Museum Q7834]

white, SANLC escort. Officers had to ensure that labourers did not enter the houses of Europeans, nor were they to be trusted with white women. Finally, 'any native found wandering about without a pass and not under the escort of a white NCO should be returned to his unit under guard, or failing this, handed over to military police'.[19]

One official described the compounds as providing 'excellent' accommodation: '[t]he huts are of galvanized iron, wooden ceilings and boarded floors, and furnished with heating stoves. Washing and bathing accommodation as well as change and drying rooms are provided'.[20]

While accommodation may have been comfortable, Lieutenant-Colonel Godfrey Godley, second-in-command of the SANLC, is remarkably candid, given his position, about the nature of the compounds in a letter he wrote home during his time with the corps in France: 'the conditions of our men in France as regards freedom of movement are similar to those applying to prisoners of war, and the camps occupied by our men and prisoners of war are identical in every respect', except that the 'locality of those occupied by the prisoners are in the majority of cases more favourably situated'.[21]

Added to the very practical measures put in place to control the black members of the SANLC, Colonel Pritchard published his approach to eliciting the best possible work and behaviour from SANLC members in a pamphlet produced by the Committee for the Welfare of Africans in Europe. His philosophy was based on the belief that the South African 'native' was simple, childlike and in need of firm supervision. The pamphlet states:

The success of the African Labour Corps is to be found in the adoption of two or three very practical methods ... the firm decision to avoid any form of compulsion and only to accept *bona fide* volunteers was far-reaching in its effects. The African, in his present stage of development, does not stand compulsion at all well, for he is so much the simple child of Nature that compulsion frequently spells complete loss of energy and a high sickness and death rate. ... Col Pritchard and his colleagues have adopted and insisted upon general recognition of certain excellent methods of administration. First ... is that of believing the very best of their men, and letting them know that both as regards the discharge of their duties and their general behaviour the Africans are expected to be no less diligent in their work and no less free from misconduct than the European subjects of the King. Next ... is an insistence that the white officers must watch over the clothing of the units with scrupulous care. If a Company is found wearing damp clothes a change is immediately ordered, because damp, not cold, is a most insidious foe to the health of the African race. Mental, no less than physical, health is vital to the efficiency and comfort of labourers. The African is one of the most joyous creatures on God's earth; he loves the song and dance, and given time and opportunity to play there be little concern over the discharge of reasonable duties. Thus one of the first objects of the officers and chaplains has been that of providing every possible means for physical, mental and religious exercises.[22]

Daily life in the SANLC

The SANLC in France was deployed to a number of tasks. Forestry, to supply timber for use at the front (to buttress trenches and for the duckboards that lined the bottom of trenches, for example) and elsewhere, has already been mentioned. The corps also dug trenches, repaired and built roads – nearly 4,500 miles of roadway had to be constructed and maintained in the Lines of Communication behind the Western Front[23] – repaired railway lines and even undertook salvage work (Fig 6.6). Many of the labourers had experience working in South Africa's gold mines, which meant that they were familiar with the use of dynamite, a skill that was usefully deployed in stone quarries in Northern France. The bulk of the work of the corps, however, was related to the loading and unloading of supplies, both at railheads in the army areas and at the major ports on Normandy's Channel coast.

As was mentioned in Chapter 2, to maintain a single army division in the field required 200 tons of supplies every day. By 1918, the total weekly tonnage moving through the French Channel ports was 175,000 tons, and 1,800 trains ran every week, carrying 400,000 tons of materiel, all of which had to be loaded and unloaded by hand.[24]

The acute shortage of Allied shipping by the last year of the war meant that a rapid turnaround in French ports was essential if the supplies

Fig 6.6 Salvaging engine parts. [© Imperial War Museum Q8824]

demanded were going to continue reaching the fighting troops at the rate required to sustain them. Labour was therefore concentrated around the ports and this included numerous companies of the SANLC, which were based at Rouen, Le Havre and Dieppe.

A typical day in most SANLC camps would have followed the same general pattern:

05h30	Trumpeter's reveille (wake-up call)
06h00	Breakfast
06h45	Ration issue
07h00	Working parties fall in
07h30	General fatigues
08h30	Sick parade
13h00	Dinner (1 hour)
17h30	Return to camp

The work of the SANLC was widely complimented, and all reports about the corps indicated that it had performed exceptionally well. Although the men had a preference for forestry work, it was reported that 'in loading and unloading of stores to and from ships and trains ... they did exceptionally good work and frequently put up remarkable records', on one occasion moving nearly 170 tons of grain in an hour.[25]

Leisure and relaxation

According to the same pamphlet by the Committee for the Welfare of Africans in Europe referred to above, when the work of the day was over, the men of the SANLC 'smoke or sing together or laboriously copy English words on their slates. They have a simple child-like trust in the white officers, who talk to them in their own language, and their one desire is to do what they can to help in the war. They dig a ditch or mend a road or build a hut with a cheerful willingness'.[26]

Because the men were compounded, 'healthy relaxation' was seen as important, and leisure time was organised into 'periodical sports ... at which they ran races, jumped, threw the cricket ball, pulled tug-o-war ... and altogether used up their superfluous energy' (Fig 6.7).[27] Pritchard described various 'sports, games, studies, music and picture shows' that the SANLC men could participate in, which were made possible by the 'chaplains and certain officers of the Corps' as well as through the 'very liberal assistance [of] the London Committee for the Welfare of Africans in Europe.'[28] Official reports therefore paint a picture of contentment within the SANLC, despite the hard work the men undertook every day and their virtual imprisonment in the closed compounds.

Fig 6.7 Tug-o'-war. [© Imperial War Museum Q2384]

Surviving letters from SANLC members in the archives are also effusively positive about the life and experiences of corps members. One corps member working at Le Havre wrote:

> We are still well here every one of us, Macosini, the other Qumbu men and myself. It is now mid-summer and the country is very pretty, robed with beautiful verdure. France is a wooded country and its climate very healthy. The weather now is very much satisfaction to us ... The French are industrious people in a great measure and if the native there would work half as much as these people, South Africa would have been a very rich country ... What is most wonderful here is the beautiful twilight of this country. At 9 o'clock in the middle of the night you can sit outside and read a book.[29]

Corporal A K Xabanisa (No. 6246) of 11 Company, in a letter to the Chief Magistrate of Umtata, says:

> In view of the fact that the Government may still require some more of our people to come over to serve in France, I have deemed it prudent to inform you that in case some false information might have been told to our people of ill treatment I contradict them with facts that we have been well cared for by our officers inasmuch that some of our people who have been found medically unfit have been repatriated and every plan has been adopted to forbid us from wasting money on luxuries, which steps we will only be too

thankful for on our return. Furthermore although we were not sent to dock work every care has been taken to keep us far from accidents ... The winter was very severe but it has been admitted that such winter has not been experienced for the last thirty years ... We intend re-engaging and in fact to remain as long as the Government desires our services.[30]

These letters need to be treated cautiously, however. As mentioned already, positive letters were requested by the Government as an aid to recruitment and it is likely that only these, of the many letters sent from the SANLC to their families in South Africa, made it first past the censors and then into the surviving documentary record of the corps.

The reports of the fun and games had by the SANLC should also be viewed in the context of the closed-compound system and the extreme control imposed on the men of the corps. Although it cannot be said that enjoyment was not altogether experienced during such events, Grundlingh argues that in the 'restricted and regulated environment of the SANLC compounds, sport was not a spontaneous activity initiated by the workers themselves. It was an organized, structural affair, dictated from above and intended to function as a mechanism of control'. These activities served as a pressure-release mechanism for men confined, even during their leisure time, under an abnormal and unnatural system.[31]

In addition to the other activities offered, the authorities organised the performance of traditional African dances (Fig 6.8), to which large numbers of mainly white guests were invited. Photographs, taken at

Fig 6.8 *Performance of traditional African dances by SANLC members on the dunes at Dannes. [© Imperial War Museum Q2387]*

Dannes, show these dances, with crowds of uniformed white soldiers lining the dunes. In addition to providing a physical outlet to potential frustrations at their effective incarceration, the dances may have served a public relations use, providing a display of '"happy" and "exuberant" black "warriors", obviously "contented" with the conditions and circumstances which the authorities had created for them'.[32]

The dances and physical activities were not really popular among the workers and only a minority participated. Perhaps this is not surprising, given the physical nature of the daily work in which the SANLC was engaged. When at their leisure, most men preferred to relax, sitting around their fires talking and smoking.[33]

Educational classes, where labourers were instructed in reading and writing, translation, arithmetic and geography in the evenings after work, were another matter and were well attended, perhaps because they were presented by black chaplains and teachers – men like Isaac Dyobha – rather than organised and imposed by the white officers. Their popularity may also have been grounded on the possibility they offered corps members for self-advancement – one of the key selling points of the SANLC scheme for many of the educated black middle class who supported it from its inception.[34]

The health of the corps

The health of SANLC members while overseas was generally good. Initially, there were complaints by officials in France that the medical screening of recruits in South Africa was not being properly carried out, with many arriving in France too old for the work required, or suffering from malaria, tuberculosis, miner's phthisis[35] or even leprosy. This was quickly addressed by a nationwide telegram from the Department of Native Affairs to recruiters, insisting that the medical officers who examined recruits follow proper procedures to ensure that 'only those who are free from defects both physical or otherwise are passed'.[36]

There had been a good deal of concern, used by some opposed to the scheme to argue against it, that black South Africans' health would suffer, unaccustomed as they were to the winter cold of northern France. The fact that many men who enlisted came from the Transvaal Highveld,[37] the Orange Free State and Lesotho, where winters can be as harsh as those in France, was conveniently forgotten.

Consultations with medical experts by the Government suggested that, with proper care and close attention to clothing and hygiene, a sickness rate of between 40 and 50 men per thousand (ie 4–5 per cent) could be expected in northern France during the winter months. Although this figure would have been considered high in normal industrial conditions in South Africa, the exceptional circumstances in which the corps was to be employed led the South African authorities to conclude that medical concerns did not justify the abandonment of the scheme.[38]

Table 6.1 Monthly sick rates in five companies of SANLC at Rouen (July 1917–July 1918)[39]

Month	Average daily sick parade	Total admitted to Detention Hospital during month	Transferred to No 1 Native Labour Hospital during month	Remarks
1917				
July	-	49	29	29 cases of scurvy
August	-	55	9	
September	21	29	9	
October	45	46	13	
November	26	169	20	Departure of old companies and arrival of new companies
December	40	137	31	Frost and snow frequent
1918				
January	62	240	116	Mild damp weather Mumps
February	60	234	74	Mild damp weather Mumps and measles
March	62	226	151	Mild damp weather Mumps and measles
April	50	154	55	Weather fine. Scurvy
May	62	220	61	Influenza epidemic
June	27	78	30	
July	25	56	10	

Chilblains, trench foot and frostbite were the main winter medical issues experienced by the SANLC in France, with several men losing limbs to the latter.[40] Tuberculosis was a constant problem, and the corps also experienced a number of cases of scurvy. Table 6.1 shows the monthly sick rates for five SANLC companies (ie 2,000 men) at Rouen, for the year between July 1917 and July 1918.

Based on these figures for sickness in just this small portion of the SANLC, the predicted daily sickness rates were higher than the actual rates recorded.

The cases of scurvy in April 1918 may be accounted for by their appearance at the tail end of winter, when fresh greens and vegetables would have been difficult to obtain. Those in July of the previous year, at the height of summer, are less easy to explain but could simply be the result of a wartime diet low in vitamin C.

The outbreak of influenza in May 1918 is also intriguing, especially when viewed in light of the fact that the SANLC companies in Rouen were working in close proximity to units of the Chinese Labour Corps. Although the great influenza pandemic of 1918–19 is not usually mentioned in the medical histories of the First World War, it was a very real issue during the closing stages of the war. The Western Front was a crucible for disease, driven by the convergence there, under extreme conditions, of a mass of humanity, and in 1918, the medical services in northern France were forced to watch helplessly as this unprecedented new flu carried off healthy young soldiers in droves. Medical researchers have now succeeded in reconstructing the 1918 virus and, although uncertainties remain, their evidence suggests that it was an avian flu virus from northern China, carried to North America and Europe by members of the Chinese Labour Corps.[41]

Overall, the mortality rate within the SANLC was low. Of the 21,000 men who enlisted, 331 (1.5 per cent) died while in service, the majority from pulmonary diseases, mainly tuberculosis. A small number of men died while on their way to France. Records for HMT *Nestor*, for example, list the deaths of three black labourers: two through illness and one, Private Mack Nalana of 26th Company, who was lost overboard.[42]

Exposure to enemy fire

The SANLC's time in the army areas prior to March 1917 is likely to have left a lasting impression on the men for another reason: the apparent frequency of their exposure to enemy fire.

The following extracts from the war diaries of the C and B Companies, 2nd Battalion paint an interesting picture, and one that the South African authorities were probably keen to downplay:

24/12/1916	The O/C 'C' Coy reported that the following man had been slightly wounded by shrapnel while at work on railway construction: No 2705 Pte Simon.
18/01/1917	Lt Robinson reports that natives working on Railway Construction on the 17th were badly shelled and had to leave their work.
19/01/1917	Capt Kay reports that one native killed and another wounded by shellfire. Natives belonging to 'C' Coy again subjected to shellfire while working on Railway Construction 'ANNEQUIN' ... Men had to leave work.
21/01/1917	[No.] 4053 Samuel killed by shellfire on 19/01/1917.[43]

B Company, having survived their torrid voyage on the *Benguela*, had similar experiences immediately after their arrival in France in December 1917. They disembarked on the 10th, entrained for Albert and then marched to their camp at Aveluy, arriving 'all correct' on 11 December.[44] That night, and for weeks thereafter, they were subject to regular shelling while at work and within the camp. The following are extracts from the company war diary for December 1916 and January 1917:

22/12/1916	We are intentionally shelled but not very near camp.
25/12/1916	Three natives wounded by Mills Bomb in Aveluy wood.
26/12/1916	Shells fell in Aveluy.
31/12/1916	Shells fell near camp on night of 31st.
06/01/1917	Shelled in morning by hostile which fell wide of camp ... Heavily shelled around camp and Aveluy 11 pm to 1 am. Some 50 shells landed in vicinity.
08/01/1917	Shelled at 6am and 8am. Retired to dug out.
12/01/1917	At 11am the first actual shelling of camp. One shell falling between incinerators about 10 yards from OC lying with about 50 natives in Sunk Road. Natives all taken out of camp onto Sunk Road.
15/01/1917	Shelled again during day up to about 1 am.
16/01/1917	Shelled at night. Natives very panic stricken and sleeping out in open trenches.
18/01/1917	Deputation from Native Indunas re protection against shell fire.
19/01/1917	Heavy shelling at Aveluy and Camp. 18 casualties altogether. 3 killed, 15 wounded including 2 natives (one

killed No 4053 Pte Samuel of Mashashane's Location and
one slightly wounded by separate shells). The native who
was killed smashed to a pulp and had (?) in his clothes,
which were in shreds.[45]

20/01/1917   Native Samuel buried at Aveluy Cemetery ... Badly shelled
during day. 2 shells fell in camp. One hitting wire and the
other just missing hospital.

23/01/1917   Dug trenches in camp for use of natives during shelling.

24/01/1917   Badly shelled during night natives and ourselves in dug
outs. Got up 4 times during night. Bitterly cold.

26/01/1917   Shelled again during night. Natives practically all out of
Nissen huts in dug outs and trenches for 4 hours. About
50 per cent preferring to sleep on in trenches ... this in
12 degrees of frost.[46]

Later entries describe continued shelling and bombing by German
aeroplanes.

A letter, presumably from a white officer with the SANLC, provides
more detail of the events described in the war diary:

Germans shelled us intermittently for three months. One poor fellow, a
native of Mashishaan's [sic], Pietersburg District, got a direct hit from a
5.9.[47] He was blown to a pulp and we had to bury him in his clothes. One
man got wounded at another time. Three or four were saved by slid [sic]
helmets. Sometimes as many as 200 shells fell around the work where we
were but it is marvellous to relate how very few were touched. There were
plenty of narrow escapes. I must ... mention the aeroplane bombs. These
used to come on bright moonlit nights when it was bitterly cold ... we had to
get out sometimes into trenches from our warm beds 4 or 5 times at night.
Our windows were blown in by a bomb ... We saw quite a lot of warfare and
the natives especially became very smart at spotting the differences between
our guns and the enemies and the different aeroplanes.[48]

Relocation of SANLC units

Rumours about these and other incidents did filter back to South Africa
and a concerned official wrote to the Magistrate of Matatiele:

I have the honour to enquire whether Natives already attested as Dock
Labourers will be employed on other branches of work without their
consent first being obtained. Rumours ... have been current for some time
but have been contradicted by me on all possible occasions and the natives

informed that they can trust the Government to carry out to the letter their part of the agreement ... the disaffected in this district will point to this as the first step towards using the natives in the danger zone and it will become increasingly difficult to reassure them.[49]

Shortly thereafter, the Acting Director of Native Labour, E K Whitehead, sent out the following disingenuous circular to all magistrates:

As you are aware it was the intention to employ the Contingent exclusively on dock work at the French ports and to this end the natives so far recruited have been attested. Owing to various technical difficulties that have arisen and have been represented to this Government through the Secretary of State I am glad to say that it is now proposed to extend the usefulness of the Contingent by increasing the scope of employment to include roadmaking, quarrying and work incidental to forestry, all of which work it is perhaps needless to add, will be away from any danger zone. In order to meet this new position it will be necessary to amend the present contract sheet by enrolling recruits as general labourers instead of for dock work only and I would ask you to be good enough to do this as from the date of receipt of this circular minute. It is confidentially considered that the widening of the scope of employment will be welcomed by the natives and will have the effect of stimulating recruiting to a marked degree.[50]

The deployments of SANLC companies had, from the very beginning therefore, been directly contradictory to the letter and spirit of the contracts signed by those who enlisted.

The exposure to fire made many of the men of the SANLC nervous and, as shown by the war diary entry for B Company above, some of the companies petitioned to be removed from the forward areas, reminding the authorities that their contracts stated that they would be employed on dock work.

It was, therefore, agreed that the forward SANLC units would be moved back into the Lines of Communications, which commenced on 1 March 1917. Some SANLC companies 'strongly objected to their removal [which they regarded] as a slur on their character and loyalty as soldiers'.[51]

The relocation of the SANLC meant some manoeuvring and juggling of labour corps. According to the War Office's Official Report on British Foreign Labour, the presence of French Chinese labour corps south of the Somme, 'whose administration in the opinion of the British experts [was] far too lax', resulted in the relocation of the Chinese to the north and the installation of the SANLC south of the river.[52]

There was great hesitation about moving the SANLC to Havre and Rouen, where complete segregation would be difficult to maintain due to the areas being densely populated and the presence of other working parties at the docks. The 'urgency of the situation, involving the effective employment of the Chinese as well as the SANLC, and the release of British Labour Companies from the Base Ports for work in forward areas, [however] justified the overcoming of the scruples of the Staff Officer, SANLC'.[53]

The relocation of the corps to the Lines of Communication meant that after March 1917, Saigneville, Dannes, Abancourt, Audricq, Zeneghen, Rouen and Havre became the main centres of SANLC activities.[54]

7

Seaward the great ships

At the beginning of the 19th century, the tonnage of merchant ships built in Scotland was roughly equivalent to the output of one of the great English shipbuilding rivers such as the Thames or the Tyne. But during that century, Scottish shipbuilding was to play a pivotal role in British industrialisation. By the time that the *Mendi* was built in 1905, the Clyde was the greatest shipbuilding river in the world. Between 1890 and 1913, over 20 per cent of the world's new merchant ship tonnage was built on the river.[1]

Clyde shipbuilding

Prior to 1800, most of the Scottish shipbuilding industry was concentrated on the east coast, principally at Aberdeen, Leith and Dundee. In 1829, Scottish shipbuilding accounted for only 16 per cent of the output of British shipyards, just under 67,000 net tons. Clyde shipyards built about 35 per cent of this tonnage and employed about a quarter of the workforce. However, the balance was shifting westwards. By 1871, nearly 80 per cent of Scottish shipbuilders were employed on the Clyde and about 88 per cent of the tonnage built in Scotland came from Clyde yards (Fig 7.1). Furthermore, this had grown from 6 per cent to almost 30 per cent of total British output.[2]

The reasons for the dramatic growth of the Clyde shipbuilding industry during these four decades lie in the dramatic changes that transformed British industry in the 19th century. Few industries were reshaped as much as shipbuilding, which saw revolutionary changes in scale, product and technology. Wooden ships that had changed little during the previous two centuries gave way to iron ones. Sail gave way to steam and screw propellers. Specialist vessels were developed to carry different cargoes, and the size of ships increased dramatically.

By the time that the *Mendi* was built in the first decade of the 20th century, the yards of the Clyde were at their peak, dominating the Scottish shipbuilding industry. In 1911, Clyde yards were responsible for about a third of the tonnage of ships produced in Britain – almost 333,000 net

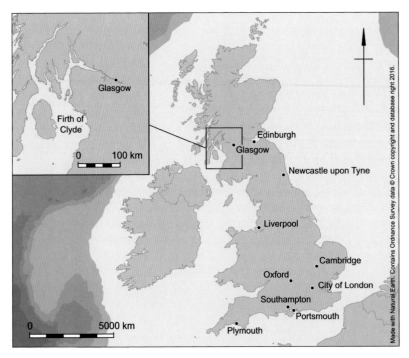

Fig 7.1 Map showing the location of the Clyde. [© Wessex Archaeology]

tons – and almost all of the tonnage built in Scotland. Steel had supplanted iron as the building material of choice.

The huge advance in Clyde shipbuilding was possible because the older Scottish system of small, and often short-lived, shipyards run by small family concerns was replaced in the 19th century by large integrated engineering establishments run by major limited companies, which had access to the large amounts of capital required. For example, the naval and liner yard built at Dalmuir in 1907 cost almost a million pounds – equivalent to about £87 million today – to set up.

Alexander Stephens

The shipbuilders of the *Mendi* were Alexander Stephen and Sons, usually referred to as Alex(ander) Stephens or even just Stephens, which had been founded in Gurghead on the Moray Firth soon after the 1745 Jacobite rebellion by Alexander Stephen, the son of a farmer. At the time, the east coast dominated Scottish shipbuilding and the new business probably concentrated on small coasters and fishing vessels. By 1813, the business was established in Aberdeen, moving in the 1840s to Dundee.

In 1850, a decisive moment in the firm's future occurred when the clearly ambitious Alexander Stephen who had acquired the firm and restored its fortunes in the 1830s and 1840s decided to establish a new yard on the Clyde, seeing there the opportunity to build iron steamships. He took over the Kelvinhaugh yard in 1851 and the firm's first iron ship, a sailing vessel, was launched in 1852. The scale of capital investment required was impressive: in 1851 a total of £18,000 (around £1,750,000 today) had been invested in the yard by both landlord and tenant.[3]

In 1869, his son, another Alexander, built a new shipyard for the construction of iron steamships at Linthouse (Fig 7.2). The move from Kelvinhaugh to Linthouse meant that for the first time the firm had its own engine house. This was purpose-built and expanded over the years, enabling the firm to build the steam reciprocating engines and Scotch marine-type boilers, as later fitted to the *Mendi*, as well as supplying other shipyards. The last two decades of the 19th century saw further growth – by the 1880s the yard had started to build in steel, launching 23,000 tons in 1888 – and also saw the firm sever its links with what was left of the east coast shipbuilding industry when their Dundee yard was sold.

Fig 7.2 Aerial photo of the Linthouse yard taken in 1928. [© Crown copyright. RCAHMS]

In 1900, Alexander Stephens became a limited company and took a deliberate decision not to compete in the pure cargo-ship market and to instead focus on liners. By the time that the *Mendi* was built in 1905, the firm had an established reputation for the high construction standards of its liners, which ensured it prestige customers, such as P&O. The firm built many of the ships that serviced the important banana trade between Britain and the West Indies, including one-third of the banana-trade fleets of the prominent shipping companies Elder Dempster and Fyffe. In 1905, Alexander Stephens built about 33,000 gross tons of ships at Linthouse and averaged about 30,000 tons in the 10 years prior to 1914, ensuring the firm's place in the first rank of Clyde shipbuilders. The First World War had a dramatic impact upon Alexander Stephens: from 41,000 tons built in 1914, and a full order book, the Linthouse yard produced no merchant tonnage at all in 1916. However, this paralysis, partly due to the enlistment of its workers, gave way to the production of naval vessels, mainly destroyers, as it became apparent that the regular warship builders could not meet demand, and the recruitment of women workers began in earnest. A significant number of military aircraft were also built at Linthouse, including the famous BE.2 two-seater.

Alexander Stephens survived the inter-war booms and busts of the shipping industry and played a very active role in supplying new tonnage during the Second World War. In the post-war years, the firm followed a strategy of competing for high-quality work and diversified into ship repair. However, by the mid-1960s, the firm was experiencing the general financial difficulties being faced by other yards on the Clyde, and in 1976, the Stephen family finally disposed of the last vestiges of their business. The Linthouse yard, which had already been closed, was demolished in the late 1980s. The engine shop was transported piece by piece to the Scottish Maritime Museum at Irvine.

Cargo liners

Many of the vessels built by Stephens in the late 19th and early 20th centuries, including the *Mendi*, were 'cargo liners'. Unlike 'tramp steamers', which carried bulk cargoes and sailed whenever these became available to wherever they had to go, cargo liners operated a long-distance trade to named destinations on a regular schedule.

Cargo liners were first introduced in the mid-19th century for the trade between Britain and the Far East, and the development of more efficient compound engines, increase in ship size and the opening of the two major 'shortcuts' of world trade – the Suez and Panama Canals – enabled these

Fig 7.3 Typical cargo liner.

steam-driven vessels to challenge the commercial dominance of sail on even the longest routes (Fig 7.3).

Cargo liners carried a very wide variety of goods, which inevitably reflected patterns of trade in the colonial world of the time, and these ships therefore came to be regarded as a backbone of the Empire. They carried manufactured goods from industrialised nations to their colonies on the outward voyage, and raw materials for those manufacturing industries and foodstuffs for their workers on the return voyage. Manufactured goods of every kind were carried, from screws to railway engines. Foodstuffs included cereals, fruit, livestock, sugar and beverages such as tea and coffee. The introduction of on-board refrigeration plants from the 1880s also meant that they could carry frozen meat and dairy products over long distances.[4]

The sheer variety of goods carried meant that the cargo space was more divided than in tramp ships, so a cargo liner often had several holds and these were usually subdivided horizontally by 'tween decks. Cargo liners also tended to be well endowed with their own derricks and winches to handle cargo. These were particularly important for those ships calling regularly at smaller colonial ports, which were often only very basically equipped.

Passengers were attracted to cargo liners because they operated to fixed schedules and called at many more ports than the larger specialist passenger liners. As a result, passenger accommodation, which was often quite luxurious, was usually provided in the design of these ships.

In the early 20th century, cargo liners might carry significant numbers of passengers – in the case of the *Mendi*, up to 170 – although later regulation considerably reduced the number of passengers that could be accommodated. The advantages appreciated by passengers were also attractive to those shipping mail, with the result that postal services came to rely on the cargo liner for the carriage of letters and parcels.

The carriage of perishable goods and passengers put a premium on speed. While cargo liners were generally slower than passenger liners, they were normally faster than tramp ships and, in the first decade of the 20th century, could typically sustain a speed of 11 or 12 knots. In the 1880s, the introduction of triple-expansion reciprocating steam engines, such as the engine carried by the *Mendi*, represented a major leap forward in the fuel efficiency of steam engines and therefore also in the economic viability of the cargo liner. The widespread adoption for merchant ships of the next major pre-First World War advances in propulsion – steam turbines and diesel engines – came too late to influence the design of the *Mendi*, even though Alexander Stephen and Sons had built a turbine-driven yacht in 1903.[5]

Building the *Mendi*

The *Mendi* was launched on 19 June 1905 (Fig 7.4). It was a sister ship of the *Karina*, launched by the same yard for the same clients in the same year. Information about the design of the *Mendi*, which was a development from the ships of the earlier *Zungeru* class, is available from a number of sources, including the particulars contained in the official registry, the plans of Alexander Stephens, the Board of Trade Inquiry report into the ship's loss and a number of photographs.

The ship was 370.2 feet (112.8m) long, had a maximum breadth of 46.2 feet (14.1m) and a depth of hold of 26.96 feet (8.2m). It had a 'straight' bow, meaning it had only a very slight rake or lean forward and an overhanging 'elliptical' stern, designed to maximise deck space at the stern.

The *Mendi* was recorded as being 'clincher built' of steel, which meant that the many individual steel 'shell plates' used to build the hull of the ship were overlapped. This enabled them to be securely joined using rivets, welding being not yet in widespread use for shipbuilding. Photographs of the ship suggest that this was done using the normal 'in-out' system, whereby one strake (line) of plates was lapped over, the one below that lapped under, the one below over and so on.

Propulsion was supplied by three triple-expansion steam engines that were fitted amidships. These direct-acting engines produced 654 nominal horse power.[6] The cylinders of the engine were mounted vertically

Fig 7.4 British & African Steam Navigation Company postcard showing the Mendi.

and operated inverted, so that the steam pressure pushed the pistons downwards. They drove a single 'screw' propeller at the stern via a long propeller shaft. The sustained speed that could be achieved by the *Mendi* was reported by the Inquiry to have been 13 knots. A simple steam engine relies on the expansion of steam drawn into a closed cylinder to push a piston along the cylinder, which turns a crank and, in the case of a ship, then turns a shaft, which turns a propeller. However, the expanding steam cools and condenses, thus reducing the efficiency of the engine on the next stroke. Compounding involves expanding the steam in a number of stages, reducing the temperature loss on each expansion and therefore the amount of condensation, and thus producing a much more efficient engine. Triple expansion involves three stages and therefore three cylinders and pistons. These are of different sizes, with the largest-diameter cylinder being used for the low-pressure expansion (the pistons of the *Mendi* were 29, 46 and 77 inches – 74, 117 and 196 centimetres – in diameter).

The widespread introduction of compounding in the second half of the 19th century greatly improved the commercial viability of steam ships by dramatically reducing coal consumption. Crucially, this enabled them to gradually replace sailing ships on long-distance trade routes. The first patent for a compound engine was taken out by Charles Randolph and John Elder in 1853 and the first trial of their engine in the Alexander Stephens-built *Brandon* the following year produced a saving in coal of 30 per cent. This was developed into an effective triple-expansion engine by A C Kirk at John Elder and Co at Govan on the Clyde in the 1870s, saving another 20 per cent. Although quadruple expansion was developed for the very largest merchant ships, the engines of the *Mendi* nevertheless represent the fully mature marine steam engine.

The *Mendi*'s engines were supplied with steam at 180lb (82kg) by four cylindrical steel boilers. The basic operating principle of marine boilers such as these was fairly simple. Each was essentially a large water tank with a number of furnaces at its base. The hot gases from coal burnt in the furnaces had to be vented. On their way to the funnel, these gases were passed through tubes in the water tank. This process, and the radiant heat from the furnace, heated the water in the tank, creating pressurised steam, which was then conveyed by pipes to the engines. Although early boilers were flat sided and therefore space saving, it soon became apparent that cylindrical boilers were stronger and therefore better suited to high pressures.

The *Mendi*'s boilers were of the 'Scotch' type. These were developed by the Glasgow engineer James Howden in the 1860s and represent another of the Clyde's great contributions to marine engineering. They were the most common steam generators in merchant service during the era of triple expansion, which depended upon a higher steam pressure than had been required by earlier engines (compounding requires steam pressures above 40psi). The use of steel, and improvements in steel quality, enabled these boilers to cope with the high pressures required, although the boiler-plate thickness required to ensure sufficient strength meant that boiler weight was always an issue for naval architects. The increased size necessary to ensure that sufficient steam was available also meant that the boiler rooms and their associated vent trunking occupied a greater proportion of the space available within a ship, inevitably occupying valuable cargo and passenger space. To minimise the size of boilers required, and also to allow lower-quality and cheaper coal to be used, ships such as the *Mendi* were fitted with equipment to pressurise and therefore increase the amount of air going into the boilers. These 'forced-draught' systems usually heated the air by passing it over or through hot exhaust gases that were channelled up the funnels.[7]

The space within the ship was divided transversely by a total of six watertight bulkheads, forming a series of compartments below the upper deck (Figs 7.5 and 7.6). These bulkheads were part of the watertight subdivision of the ship and were intended to prevent the whole of the ship flooding if there was a hole in the hull. They also contributed to the ship's structural strength.

The amidships compartment contained the ship's engine and boilers. On either side of this were two holds, with the two largest, hold nos. 1 and 2, forward and hold nos. 3 and 4 aft. Each hold was subdivided horizontally by a 'tween deck. These allowed different layers of cargo to be carried, which made the use of space within the holds much more efficient. This characteristic of cargo liners led to their often being called 'tweendeckers'. In addition, there were various spaces under and around

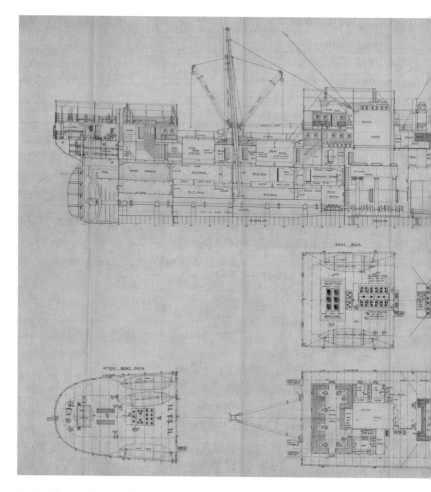

Fig 7.5 (above) Schematic drawing from ship plan showing the position of bulkheads in relation to holds and other internal spaces. [© National Maritime Museum, Greenwich, London]

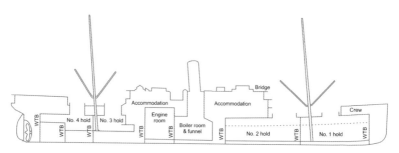

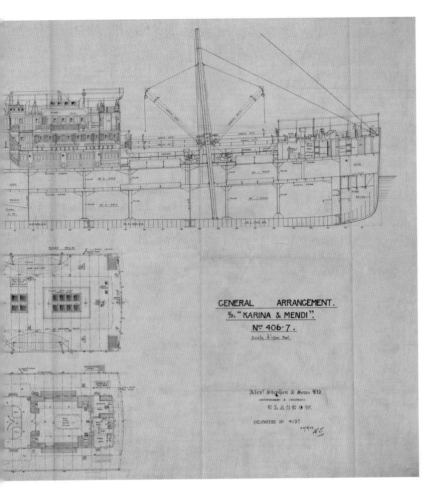

GENERAL   ARRANCEMENT.
⁵⁄ₛ "KARINA & MENDI".
N⁰ 406-7.

Fig 7.6 (opposite page, below) Plan of the Mendi *showing the arrangement of decks and bulkheads. [© Wessex Archaeology]*

the holds that were used as coal bunkers, ballast tanks, stores and for the chain locker, which stored the anchor chains when not in use. The 'tween decks formed part of what Alexander Stephens called the main deck, a series of decks between the watertight bulkheads (Fig 7.7). This was subdivided into a number of compartments, including bunkers for coal storage and various food and drink stores.

Above the holds, the upper deck ran the full length of the ship. This accommodated first- and second-class passenger cabins, together with crew accommodation and various service facilities. Above the upper deck

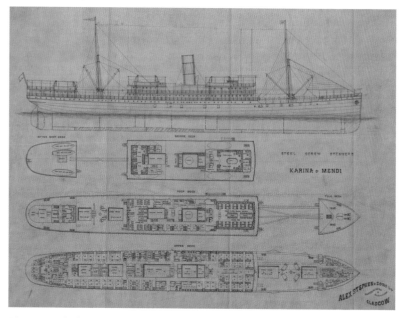

Fig 7.7 Detail of deck plans. [© National Maritime Museum, Greenwich, London]

at the bow was a small forecastle deck. The enclosed forecastle formed by these decks accommodated the ordinary crewmen.

The decks of the *Mendi* had a sheer, meaning that they rose towards the bow and stern, producing a slight concavity amidships. This would have been barely, if at all, noticeable to anyone on deck, but it had an important function in that it improved the buoyancy and stability of the ship when sailing into rough seas and reduced the amount of water breaking over the decks. The deck was also cambered, which assisted drainage. In addition to providing accommodation and walkway spaces, the decks, like the bulkheads, also provided structural strength.

Above the upper deck was the poop deck, running from above hold 2 to the stern. The dining saloons and associated facilities, including the 2nd-class smoking room, together with further crew accommodation and the ship's steering gear, were on the poop deck. As the upper deck above the forward holds was not enclosed and was therefore what is called a 'well deck', the poop deck was connected to the forecastle deck by a fore and aft 'flying bridge', or raised walkway, on the port side. The poop deck compartments were not the full width of the ship, so there was a walkway around them.

Above the poop deck at the stern was a small deck called the after boat deck, while above the poop deck amidships there was a bridge deck, in two parts, fore and aft of the single funnel. The edges of this deck were supported on stanchions above the poop deck walkway and there was a walkway around all sides of it. The bridge deck was connected to the aft boat deck by another fore and aft flying bridge. The bridge deck accommodated additional recreational facilities for the first-class passengers, including the music room. Above the two parts of the bridge deck were additional boat decks. The forward boat deck also accommodated the navigating bridge, with the captain's accommodation and chart room immediately below this at the forward end of the bridge deck.

The upper and poop decks were pierced amidships by the engine and boiler casings and above the holds by four cargo hatches (Fig 7.8), the largest of these being above hold 2. The hatches are described in the Inquiry as having coamings standing two feet (60cm) high above the deck. The holds were accessed from the hatches by iron-rung ladders. Wooden gratings were used to secure the hatches and these could be covered by tarpaulins and battened down in rough weather.

The *Mendi* was 'schooner rigged' with two masts, one between the hatches of hold nos. 1 and 2 and one between nos. 3 and 4. The *Mendi* was not, however, expected to sail. Instead, their principal role was as part of

Fig 7.8 Nigerian troops lounging on the hatch covers of the Mendi. *[© Imperial War Museum Q15639]*

the ship's cargo-handling equipment. The forward mast was fitted with four derricks for cargo handling and the aft with two, each of which was served by a steam-powered cargo winch. These derricks were spars with blocks and tackle that were attached to the masts and could be pivoted around to lift cargo, in much the same way as cranes. Cargo liners such as the *Mendi* needed derricks because they might have to unload their cargoes onto quaysides that lacked cranes, or into boats and barges brought alongside. It is likely that the *Mendi's* spars would have had different lifting capacities, with perhaps a couple of them being capable of handling heavy loads.

The ship was licensed to carry 100 first- and 70 second-class passengers. As well as being fitted out with sufficient cabins for these passengers and separate mess and recreation facilities, the ship also carried six lifeboats, sufficient for both passengers and crew. These were mounted on the upper decks, freeing up more deck space in the accommodation areas. This 'over-decking' was a recent innovation for passenger ships and a first for the famous Elder Dempster group of shipping companies, to which the *Mendi's* owners, the British & African Steam Navigation Company Ltd, belonged.

Crewing the *Mendi*

Cargo liners required a much larger crew than tramp ships, mainly in order to provide for the needs of the passengers. When the *Mendi* left Liverpool on 22 June 1907, bound for West Africa, it was carrying a crew of 105. Of these, 19 were listed as stewards, including two stewardesses.[8]

The limited facilities at many African ports also meant that ships trading with those ports needed extra men aboard to load and discharge cargo, as well as to look after the paintwork of the ship in the corrosively humid weather conditions of West Africa. As a result, gangs of men, often from the Liberian Kroo tribe and therefore commonly known as 'Kroomen', would be taken on as temporary additions to a ship's crew and sail with it to the various African ports at which it was due to call. These 'Kroomen' might number up to 75, and additional men were also employed at the ports themselves.

The *Mendi* and West African trade

The *Mendi,* British registered as number 120875, was built for the British & African Steam Navigation Company (B&ASNC) (1900) Limited, a company based in Edinburgh, and it remained in their ownership throughout its working life. As the B&ASNC became part of the Liverpool-based Elder Dempster shipping group, the *Mendi* has always been regarded as a Liverpool ship.

In typical fashion, ownership of the *Mendi* was divided into 64 shares. The ship was mortgaged to secure it within the group and John Dempster was one of the mortgagees given an interest in the ship.[9]

The *Mendi* was built for the important West Africa trade and seems to have operated throughout its working life from that trade's chief port, Liverpool. At the beginning of the 20th century, Liverpool was one of the great ports of the world, second only to London in the British Empire, and the West Africa trade was a core element of the city's prosperity.

The trade between Liverpool and West Africa had its roots in Liverpool's commercial domination of the infamous 'triangular' or Transatlantic slave trade route of the late 18th century between Britain, Africa and the Caribbean and North America. British and other merchants working with local rulers traded in mass forced labour, devastating large parts of Africa and creating much human suffering.

Following Abolition, the British ban on the slave trade in 1807, many in Britain expected that the small British colonies that had been established in Africa to facilitate the slave trade would be relinquished. West Africa, with its unhealthy climate and warlike peoples, was seen as one of the least promising areas for expansion. However, Britain had committed itself to the ending of the slave trade and required local bases for the naval forces that were to ensure this happened. Furthermore, during the 19th century, Britain increasingly saw itself as having a duty to undertake development of tropical areas for their own 'good' and for the sake of worldwide economic development, a doctrine subsequently and famously espoused by Lord Lugard as the 'dual mandate' idea.[10] This 'duty' was fuelled by self-interest, as the British saw the African continent as an enormous reservoir of largely untapped natural resources. As a result, rather than contracting, the British colonial presence in West Africa greatly expanded.

In the late 19th and early 20th centuries, the British Empire was essentially a commercial entity, with the acquisition of colonies heavily influenced by patterns of trade and the need to secure both trade and resources by territorial control. While it remains a matter of debate as to just how important trade was in driving the transition from trading posts to colonies in West Africa in the 19th century, it was certainly a significant factor (Fig 7.9).

Nigeria was the most important of the British colonies in West Africa. In 1880, the colonial presence was limited to a very small colony centred on Lagos, but by 1914, the colony covered the area that was to become the modern post-independence state. During this period, the economy grew rapidly, achieving an annual growth rate of 26 per cent, albeit from a

Fig 7.9 B&ASNC poster. [Courtesy of Bjorn Larsson]

very low base. Exports were dominated by raw materials, principally palm kernels, palm oil and rubber. Imports were for the most part manufactured goods, particularly cotton goods, alcohol and items made from iron or steel. Nigeria's chief trading partner was Britain, accounting for 60 per cent of its exports and over 75 per cent of its imports in 1912.[11]

The Gold Coast, modern-day Ghana, depended even more heavily on trade with Britain, with almost 65 per cent of its cocoa, gold and palm kernels going to British ports and 89 per cent of its imports coming from them.[12] Again, it was a raw materials out, manufactured goods in trade, and, while its trade grew at a similarly rapid rate, the economy that developed was likewise unbalanced. The result was that Britain's West African colonies saw little development beyond what was necessary to maintain and defend the efficient production of raw materials. This was particularly noticeable at the West African ports, which very largely failed to develop significant industrial hinterlands prior to independence.

Liverpool merchants saw an opportunity to exploit the commercial experience of West Africa that they had developed before Abolition by developing a lucrative trade in non-human cargoes. By degrees, Liverpool came to dominate this trade, and maintained its position as its leading port until after the Second World War.

The *Mendi* was typical of the cargo liners deployed in this trade by Liverpool ship owners. Surviving Board of Trade inwards passenger lists[13] indicate that it made 53 scheduled round trips between Liverpool and regular ports of call in West Africa between 1906 and 1916, an average of five to six per year. Unfortunately, little remains of the Elder Dempster archive for the period before 1932 and it is not therefore possible to know what exactly was shipped along with the passengers.

The outbreak of the First World War had a number of impacts upon the trade in which the *Mendi* was engaged, although the ship seems to have remained busy. Exports to Britain were affected by higher shipping costs, partly as a result of a shortage of ships caused by increased demand, war requisitions and losses. From 1916, the British Government also sought supplies from the cheapest, and therefore usually the nearest, markets, and the trade experienced distortions in demand caused by a shift from civilian to military production. The value of both imports and exports more than doubled during the war years, although the extent to which this was a physical increase rather than price inflation is not clear.[14]

8

The last voyage of the *Mendi*

The *Mendi* becomes a troopship

Under the command of Captain Henry Arthur Yardley, the *Mendi* and its crew left Liverpool for the last time on 11 October 1916, bound for West Africa carrying cargo. The ship had been chartered by the British Government for war service that autumn and took with it fittings for conversion into a troopship (Fig 8.1). After the ship had arrived safely at Lagos in the British colony of Nigeria and unloaded the final part of its cargo, the conversion work was carried out.

While no plans or photographs of the interior of the ship after conversion exist, the written report of the Board of Trade Court of Inquiry into the subsequent loss of the ship gives a fairly good understanding of what was done. Holds 1, 2 and 4 were each fitted with additional decks within the holds. By providing extra deck space, these maximised the number of troops that could be carried in each hold. Nothing is known about the design of these decks, but as they were intended to be temporary, they were probably mainly made of wood. Embarked troops would have sheltered or slept in the holds during cold or bad weather and would have kept their equipment there. Hold 3 was reserved for cargo.

There were no doors in the bulkheads between holds 1 and 2. As existing access from the open decks into each hold was limited to a narrow ladder bolted onto the bulkheads, a wide staircase-like ladder was fitted in each hold. This was accessed through a small 'booby hatch' in the starboard corner of each hatch cover. As hold 2 was larger, and therefore expected to accommodate more men, two ladders were fitted. It was not expected that the officers or, in the case of colonial units, white NCOs, would be accommodated in the holds: they and any civilian passengers being carried would have used the existing accommodation, the first- and second-class cabins.

The *Mendi* embarked men of the Nigerian Regiment at Lagos and Calabar before sailing via Cape Town to Dar-es-Salaam in German East Africa. At the time, Britain and South Africa were fighting a bitter and long-running campaign against German and African troops defending the German colony. One of the officers of the regiment, Lieutenant L A W Powell, had a camera with him and photographed the men of the regiment

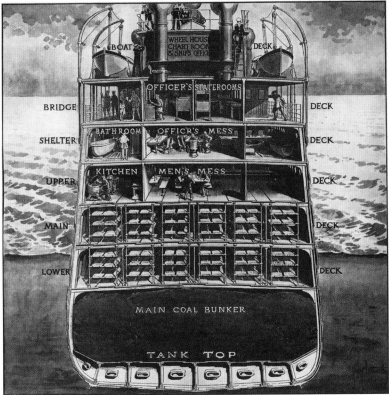

Fig 8.1 Representation of the arrangement of a typical troopship during World War One. [The Graphic, *October 21, 1916, p 481*]

embarking at Calabar and relaxing on deck (Fig 8.2). No doubt the atmosphere within the holds would have been both hot and stale and it is quite likely that the troops slept on deck when they could. The troops were then disembarked before the ship sailed south again to Cape Town via Durban. There it prepared for its last voyage to Le Havre in France, which it would reach via West Africa and Plymouth.

Fig 8.2 Looking aft, these Nigerian troops are lounging on the hatch covers of holds 3 and 4 of the Mendi. *[© Imperial War Museum Q015592]*

Captain Yardley of the *Mendi*

Henry Arthur Yardley (Fig 8.3) was born in April 1862 in the Midlands, the son of Henry and Elizabeth Yardley and one of six children. His was probably not a seafaring family: his father is recorded as being a poultry dealer.

Yardley first went to sea when he was apprenticed to a London shipping firm. His early career was on sailing ships and he voyaged as far as the East Indies. After rising to the rank of second mate, he was shipwrecked on a coral reef in the South Pacific. Taking charge of one of the two lifeboats, he guided it and the survivors to the safety of Tahiti. On his return, he joined a Liverpool shipping firm before gaining his Certificate of Competency as an Extra Master on 15 June 1889. This was the highest level of professional qualification in the British Merchant Marine and a remarkable achievement for someone so young and self-tutored. In 1892, he joined Elder Dempster and was appointed to the command of a steamship in 1898. He went on to command the *Mendi* and other ships on the West Africa trade.

Fig 8.3 Captain Henry Arthur Yardley, photographed at a later stage in his career at sea. [© Liverpool Museums Maritime Archives, Elder Dempster Collection]

The only surviving photographs of Yardley are from much later in his career and in black and white, but his pass certificate for Master in 1888 described him as 5 ft 10½in (1.8m) tall, of dark complexion, with brown hair, grey eyes and a scar on his right wrist. He married in 1897 and, after moving to Liverpool, he and his wife, Ada, had a son, whom they named Henry.

A diverse crew

On its last voyage, the ship seems to have been carrying a smaller crew than would have been normal before the war. This may have been due to the lack of paying passengers and perhaps the difficulties of finding enough men during the war. Most of the crew would have been in their usual berths in the forecastle, whereas the cabins of the ship's officers were among or near the passenger accommodation. For example, the cabin of the ship's purser, Smith, with its steel safe and barred portholes, is marked on the ship plans on the poop deck. Captain Yardley's cabin and his chart room were below the navigating bridge to enable him to reach the helm and engine controls quickly.

Altogether, the *Mendi* carried a crew of 89. In addition to Captain Yardley, there were four other ship's officers. A chief engineer was responsible for engineering and had the help of five other engineers. For handling the ship, there were, in descending order of seniority, five able-bodied seamen, one ordinary seaman, two deck hands and two deck boys. The 'below-deck' seamen comprised three 'greasers', whose job it was to keep the machinery of the ship lubricated, as well as nine trimmers, who supplied 10 firemen with coal with which to stoke the boiler fires – both back-breaking jobs.

The needs of the crew and passengers were looked after by a small army of people, including an overall chief steward, three more chief stewards, eight stewards, 15 assistant stewards, a storekeeper, a barber, a chef, two cooks, a baker and an assistant baker, a butcher and a scullion, who carried out menial work in the kitchen. The ship also carried a surgeon, a purser, a telegraphist, a carpenter, a boatswain and a quartermaster.

There were at least 25 Africans among the crew – chiefly from Sierra Leone, Benin and Nigeria (although as they had Anglicised names, it is hard to know where exactly they originated from) – who worked as deckhands, firemen, trimmers and in the galley. The work of 26-year-old Sierra Leonean Thomas Williams as a fireman and 19-year-old J James from Benin as a trimmer were typical of the roles of Africans on board ships such as the *Mendi*.

Nearly all the rest of the crew – including all the senior officers and most of the skilled crew such as cooks and those looking after the passengers, the stewards – were white British. However, there were also some other Europeans working on board: the 45-year-old carpenter, Olsson, was Swedish; the 23-year-old lamp trimmer, Hougaard,[1] was Danish; and there were two Russians – the 29-year-old 5th engineer Messner and the 23-year-old able seaman Nok. Messner's name suggests that his family had German origins and it is possible that he could have been from the Baltic coast of Russia, the area now occupied by Poland, Estonia, Latvia and Lithuania.

The SANLC embarks

In Cape Town, after an overhauling of the hold accommodation, the 5th Battalion of the South African Native Labour Corps was embarked, which is why the ship was headed for Le Havre. The battalion comprised five officers, 17 non-commissioned officers – all white – and 802 enlisted labourers. The labourers were accommodated in the holds, the white officers and non-commissioned officers in the passenger cabins.

A number of other military passengers, including officers returning to Europe after being wounded in the East Africa campaign and a group of men selected for service in the Royal Flying Corps, also joined the ship. The *Mendi* also loaded 1,500 tons of government freight, including a £5 million consignment of South African gold.

Among the men of the SANLC waiting for the *Mendi* to sail was the white NCO Colour Sergeant Robert Alexander MacTavish (Fig 8.4), who wrote to his wife from the ship just before it sailed:

Table Bay
Tuesday 16 January 17

Dear Bert
Just a line while still waiting to leave to again wish you goodbye. When I got the chance yesterday after all the excitement I looked in your direction. Had rather a restless night so far. This is a fine boat and nicely fitted up, two in each cabin. Suppose shall get used to my new surroundings in a day or two.

Ta ta fondest love
Bob[2]

Fig 8.4 Sergeant Robert MacTavish. [MacTavish Family Archive]

MacTavish also wrote a postcard to one of his young sons: 'This is the big ship that is taking us across the sea. Love from Daddy'.[3] The ship shown in the photograph on the other side of the card is in Table Bay at Cape Town but is not the *Mendi* (Fig 8.5). MacTavish must have realised that his son would not know the difference.

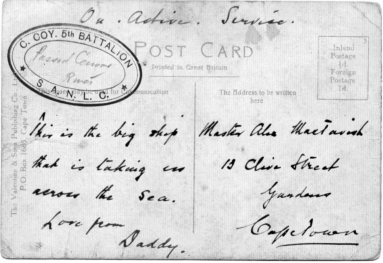

Fig 8.5 The postcard written by Sergeant MacTavish to his young son before the Mendi *sailed from Table Bay. [MacTavish Family Archive]*

MacTavish was born in Tsolo in what is now part of the Eastern Cape province of South Africa in 1873. His father was from Aberdeen in Scotland, his mother from Cork in Southern Ireland. A former Post Office clerk, he was 43 years old and left his wife, Annie Albertha ('Bert') and six children, Bob, Hugh, Sheila, Myrtle, Alex and Kenneth ('Tookie') at home.

As a lieutenant, MacTavish had volunteered for service in South-West Africa with the South African Field and Postal Corps, presumably because he already had relevant experience and skills. However, he did not actually serve there. After he was discharged, he signed up again as a colour-sergeant with the SANLC. He was prepared to forego his commission in order to do this.

Among the black South African labourers quartered in one of the *Mendi*'s holds was Private William Mathumetse, from Maleeuskop, near Groblersdal in the former Transvaal. He was only 16 years old when he enlisted in 1917. His father, Reverend Nathan Mathumetse was an early pastor of the Lutheran Church; his grandfather, Thomas Mokone, an evangelist with a reputation as a bold and fearless warrior.

William's mother was distraught when her favourite son decided to sign up and his parents therefore passed the responsibility for the decision as to whether he should go to his grandfather Thomas. William walked 30 miles to visit his grandfather, who dismissed his parents as cowards, then disappeared for a few minutes before re-emerging with a vicious-looking battle-axe. He did a war dance around the fire, swinging the axe several times over William's head, then said, 'Young man, of course you are going'.[4]

Private Sikaniso Mtolo was a married Zulu from Richmond, in what is now KwaZulu-Natal. According to his identification pass (Fig 8.6), he was 5ft 7in (1.7m) tall and 30 years old.[5] According to his grandchildren, when Mtolo left his kraal (homestead), he simply told his wife that he was leaving to look for a job.[6]

Also among the men quartered in one of the holds was Private Joseph Tshite. As a schoolmaster, Tshite was an example of the educated black elite who signed up for service with the SANLC. He was from the Hebron district of South Africa near Pretoria, where he lived with his wife and five children, including a son called Kenneth. He had enlisted with his friends Benjamin Mogorosi and Pinefas More.

Farewell to Africa

The *Mendi* left Cape Town in convoy with the *Kenilworth Castle* and other liners on 16 January 1917. The convoy was escorted by the old armoured cruiser HMS *Cornwall*, which was just as well because the convoy was sighted and shadowed on that day by the German surface raider SMS *Wolf*. The German ship would have been completely outclassed by the *Cornwall* and prudently sailed away to continue its principal mission of laying mines.

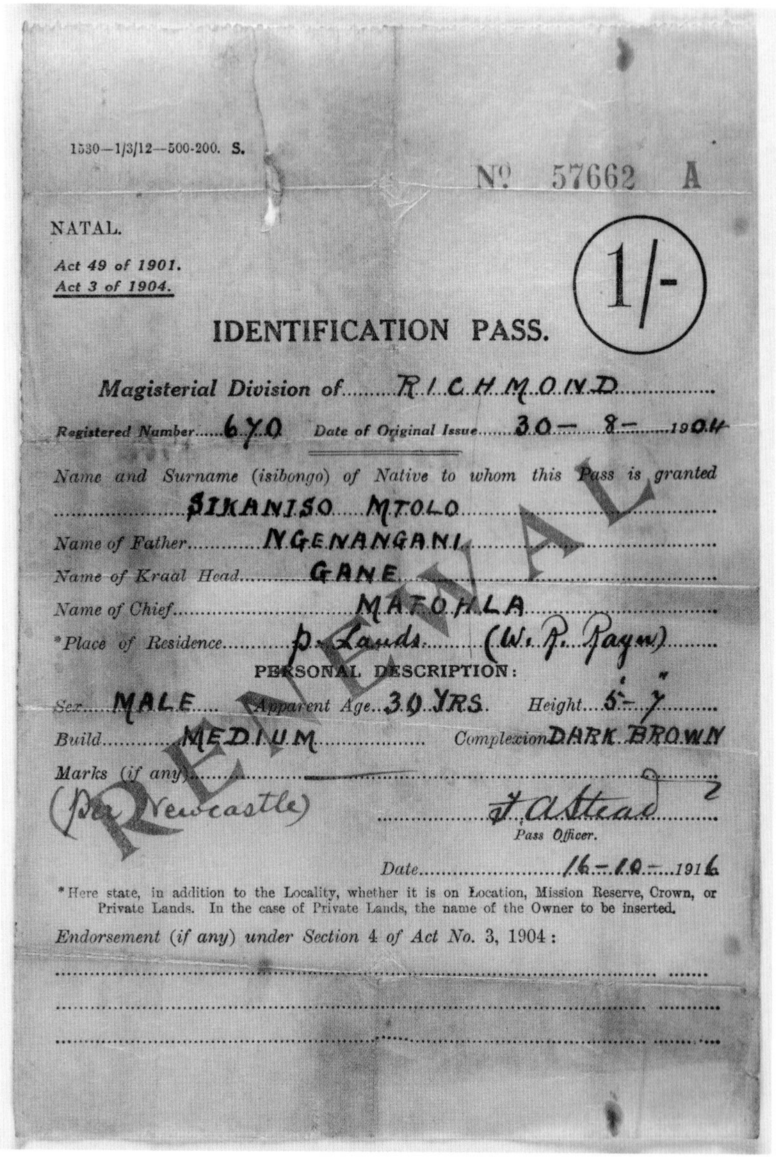
1530—1/3/12—500-200. S.

Nº 57662 A

NATAL.

Act 49 of 1901.
Act 3 of 1904.

1/-

IDENTIFICATION PASS.

Magisterial Division of R.I.C.H.M.O.N.D.

Registered Number 670 *Date of Original Issue* 30– 8– 1904

Name and Surname (isibongo) of Native to whom this Pass is granted
SIKANISO MTOLO

Name of Father NGENANGANI

Name of Kraal Head GANE

Name of Chief MATOHLA

**Place of Residence* p. Lands (W. P. Payn)

PERSONAL DESCRIPTION:

Sex MALE *Apparent Age* 30 YRS *Height* 5–7

Build MEDIUM *Complexion* DARK BROWN

Marks (if any) ——

(Per Newcastle)

REMEWAL

Pass Officer.

Date 16–10–1916

*Here state, in addition to the Locality, whether it is on Location, Mission Reserve, Crown, or Private Lands. In the case of Private Lands, the name of the Owner to be inserted.

Endorsement (if any) under Section 4 of Act No. 3, 1904:

Fig 8.6 The identification pass of Private Sikaniso Mtolo. [© Noord-Hollands Archief]

The voyage north (Fig 8.7) was otherwise uneventful. Aside from lookout duties, inspections and boat drills, there was little for the men of the SANLC to do. The white officers and NCOs were comparatively well provided for and their accounts suggest that their leisurely experience was much like that of first- and second-class passengers, albeit a little more cramped. Music and cards were played in the evening, when the ship's officers mingled with them. Complaints about the heat seem to have been

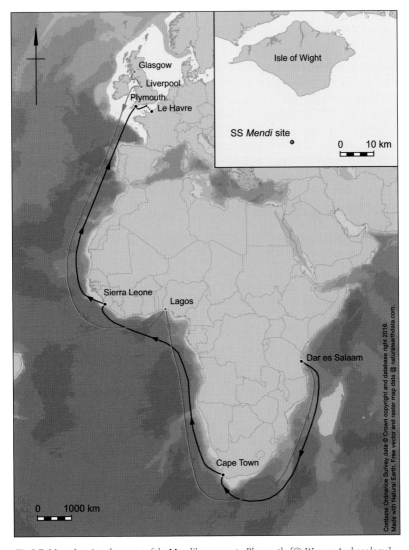

Fig 8.7 Map showing the route of the Mendi's *voyage to Plymouth. [© Wessex Archaeology]*

quite common: 38-year-old Captain Lewis Hertslet, writing to one of his daughters, mentioned that he found it particularly difficult that portholes could not be kept open for ventilation, for fear of showing a light to enemy submarines.[7] Hertslet was a medical missionary from Natal who had been asked to volunteer for the Labour Corps because he spoke Zulu. He recalled that the atmosphere was sufficiently relaxed for him to wear pyjamas in bed.

The experience of the labourers must have been rather less comfortable: they were very tightly packed in the holds – possibly in a space as small as six feet by two feet by one and a half feet (1.8 × .6 × .45m) per man[8] – and it is probable that many spent most of their time on deck. As well as drills and inspections, and the time they likely spent singing and dancing, they also apparently took part in boxing matches and evening classes, presumably organised by the officers to help keep the men busy and therefore disciplined. They also seem to have put in shifts helping the crew. Jacob Koos Matli, a young Bahaduban from near Johannesburg, described how he and his section worked a night shift as stokers later in the voyage.[9]

Many of the labourers had not seen the sea before. Most had not had the benefit of an education and their sense of wonder must have been quite profound. Private Stimela Jason Jingoes, who sailed to France with the Labour Corps on another ship, recalled his reaction and that of his comrades: 'It was the first time most of us had seen the sea, and we all spent hours talking about it and repeating, "So this is the sea!" The thing that amazed me about it was how the sun came up out of it every morning.'[10]

The convoy arrived safely in Lagos, where the bullion that the *Mendi* was carrying was transferred to the *Cornwall*. The *Mendi* then sailed to Freetown in Sierra Leona, where it waited for five days for a convoy bound for Plymouth to assemble. The convoy was to be unescorted, and during this time, therefore, a 4.7-inch gun was mounted on the stern of the ship, probably on the after boat deck.[11] The gun was served by two military gunners, one of whom was Leading Seaman William Henry Carroll, a 36-year-old Bristolian and member of the Royal Navy Reserve who had been transferred from the *Cornwall*.[12] The officers were allowed to stretch their legs ashore, but the other men of the Labour Corps were confined to the ship.

The convoy containing the *Mendi* then sailed on to Plymouth. The German submarine campaign against shipping around the British coast and in the Western Approaches as far as Portugal was intensifying and the convoy was at risk of surprise attack by torpedo and mine. During the last few days of the voyage, the weather turned cold and grey, but the convoy reached Devonport in Plymouth on 18 January without incident. The military passengers were landed, as was the battalion's Captain McLean, who was ill with appendicitis. The journey from Cape Town had taken the *Mendi* 34 days. Sergeant MacTavish took the opportunity to write to his wife from Plymouth:

18 Feby 1917

Dearest Bert

I thought on coming into Dock this afternoon that we should have an opportunity of having a look round the Town but as usual we are doomed to disappointment. Fancy even at Sierra Leone where we stayed for a week no one was allowed ashore except of course the officers. Poor Captain Maclean was taken bad with appendicitis and laid up in bed until our arrival in Plymouth where they transferred him on a stretcher ashore to Hospital to undergo an operation which I hope will be successful and that he will soon rejoin us.

I believe we sail again tomorrow for France and my only hope is that the subdued excitement or rather strain will not be as severe as it was the last few days before our arrival at Plymouth. It was a very welcome sight to see the Eddystone Lighthouse standing out in the open sea miles from anywhere and then the view of Lands End, the Lizard and Cornish Coast with the lovely houses nothing in the wooded Kloofs [valleys] very much reminding me of my first impression of leaving Fort Jackson for East London, the round hills like the Nahoon and round Cambridge. The most wonderful sight of all was to see the aeroplanes airships and seaplanes hovering over us making ... ourselves stare with mouths open then suddenly we came upon the shipping by Jove!

What a sight! Whew. As usual the cold wind nearly took the top off ones nose but we were doubly compensated to see Land once more. The trees seem to grow just by the waters edge. All the same I do not think the scenery equals the Cape. The houses here are as numerous as ant heaps and gives one the impression of their being built one on top of the other all two storied and close as sardines in a tin, the streets too are very narrow at least so they seem from the steamer.

But what a sight to see the Docks here, it seems to be nothing but a series of creeks something [like] the Buffalo River but every conceivable inch of space is utilised for some purpose or other and the houses are right down to the waters edge. I saw a very pretty church on the very top of the hill with just a few pine trees round it and it reminded me of those mentioned in words we read. I believe however the[re] is a small village lying just on the other side of the hill. It won't be long now before we reach the other coast and we all settle down to work proper. Being Sunday today makes no difference to the ordinary routine of work. I have been exceptionally busy all day with one job and another fixing up for our landing. Its extraordinary that I should still be saddled with the donkeys' share of the work. I expect its because of my willingness anyway I prefer to be busy rather than idling away my time and feeling the cold the others complain of. This evening is the first time I've put on an overcoat then only because I've a slight cold and do not care to take any risks. I often wished on this trip that I'd got a few pounds before leaving Capetown, of course poverty is no crime still its very inconvenient. I wanted to tip the stewards and sundry others but I have not got a bean and it makes me feel disinclined to go ashore when I could manage it were I differently circumstanced. Anyway I'll try tomorrow morning if only for the purpose of posting this letter. Well shall close now with fondest love to you & the children. Hoping all are well from Bob[13]

The *Kenilworth Castle* left the same day under escort and the *Mendi* was scheduled to sail to Le Havre on the following day. The route would take the ship along the south coast, past the Isle of Wight, before turning across the English Channel for its destination. However, the ship remained in port that day because the part of the route along the south coast between Plymouth and Portsmouth had been closed because of dense fog and submarine activity off Lyme Bay. The port of Le Havre was also temporarily closed due to the discovery of mines in its approaches. It was only at 00:59 on 20 February that the commander of the Devonport naval base received permission to resume sailings east of Plymouth and the *Mendi* could therefore begin the last leg of its voyage.[14]

The loss of the *Mendi*

The *Mendi* left Plymouth at 4.30 pm on an 'up-Channel' course along the south coast of England. Light winds meant that the sea was calm, but the sky was overcast and threatening mist. The danger posed by enemy submarines and the mines that they laid meant that the ship had to be escorted, and the *Mendi* was accompanied by the Royal Navy destroyer *Brisk* (Fig 8.8). Both vessels steamed at the *Mendi*'s full speed of 12 knots, the faster *Brisk* following. Several men of the Labour Corps were stationed around the ship to help the crew keep a lookout for submarines.

By 5.30 pm, it was almost dark. Dusk could be a particularly dangerous time for submarine attacks and it was not until a couple of hours later that the side and stern navigation lights were lit. Yardley insisted on oil lamps being used because he believed that they were more visible in fog than electric lights. By 11.30 pm, the weather had started to become foggy and Yardley ordered the ship's whistle to be sounded every minute to warn other ships of the *Mendi*'s presence. By midnight, the *Mendi* and *Brisk* were both reducing speed as they sailed through patches of fog, the *Brisk* a cable's length (about 180m) behind so that it could still see the stern light

Fig 8.8 HMS Brisk, *an* Acorn-*class destroyer built, like the* Mendi, *on the Clyde. [© Imperial War Museum Q75090]*

of the *Mendi*. The faster *Brisk* had difficulty in anticipating the *Mendi*'s changes in speed and struggled to maintain a safe distance.

In contrast to the first leg of the voyage, the atmosphere on board seems to have been tense. Several men of the Labour Corps were posted as guards and lookouts and passwords were required to move on deck. It was far too cold to sleep on deck and the men huddled below wrapped in their blankets. Captain Hertslet was not wearing his pyjamas anymore: when he came off watch after midnight, he slept in his clothes. Hertslet described the ship as heaving and rocking because the sea was choppy, but as the winds were light and the sea was reported by others as being smooth, it is likely that this was simply the ship rising and falling as it rode the swell often encountered in the Channel.

The fog gradually worsened, and at 3.45 am, the engines of the *Mendi* were put to slow. The whistles of other steamers could be heard some way off to starboard. Except for occasional forays down to the chart room, Yardley stayed on the bridge.

What he did not know at that time was that the course of the *Mendi* was converging with that of another ship. The steamship *Darro* (Fig 8.9), owned by the Royal Mail Steam Packet Company, had left the *Mendi*'s destination of Le Havre that evening. The *Darro* – a cargo liner like the *Mendi* but, with a gross tonnage of over 11,000 tons, more than twice as big – was carrying only cargo that had been damaged in an earlier incident.

The *Darro* and its crew of 143 were commanded by Henry Winchester Stump, an experienced master. Almost certainly worried about the

Fig 8.9 The Darro. *[Courtesy of Ditsong National Museum of Military History]*

prospects of encountering a German submarine during daylight, Stump seems to have been trying to make the English coast and relative safety by dawn. Steaming at his ship's top speed of about 14 knots, he failed to reduce speed when beset from about 11.00 pm by the same fog that had slowed the *Mendi* and the *Brisk* and defied marine regulations by failing to order the *Darro's* whistle to be sounded, although the ship did show electric navigation lights and lookouts were posted.

Shortly before 5 am, and with the *Mendi* doing between 6 and 8 knots, Yardley left his bridge to fix his position in the chart room. Over on the *Darro*, Stump and his chief officer, who had not reduced speed despite the increasingly thick fog, heard the *Mendi's* whistle and the *Brisk's* siren. The lookouts reported a green navigation light about 200 feet (60m) ahead. The order was immediately given to put the *Darro's* engines to stop and then full speed astern, and the horn was sounded. No order was given to the helm, but, with the *Mendi* just 60m ahead, there was no time to take evasive action anyway. The crew felt a violent impact almost immediately.

Over on the *Mendi*, and with Yardley away from the bridge, the 4th Officer, 35-year-old Hubert Trapnell, heard another vessel approaching. Shouting a warning to the 28-year-old 2nd Officer Herbert Raine, he sounded the whistle. Almost immediately, Trapnell saw the masthead and red portside light approaching from the starboard side. Realising the danger, Raine rang full speed astern on the engine telegraph and sounded the whistle three times. At the same time, he ordered 'hard a starboard' (the sharpest possible turn to port). But it was too late.

Yardley had heard the whistle and the telegraph and rushed back up to the bridge. As he reached it, the straight bow of the *Darro* struck the *Mendi* a very heavy right-angled blow between the forward hatches, cutting a massive hole in its side about 20 feet (6m) deep. Knocked to the deck by the force of the collision, Yardley struggled to his feet. Reaching the forward part of the bridge, he later recalled being unable to see the bow of the *Darro* because of the thickness of the fog.

The *Darro* again stopped its engines, then, after they were put to full speed astern for a couple of minutes, Stump was able to separate the two ships and the *Darro* backed away into the fog. That was the last time its crew saw the *Mendi*.

Yardley stopped the *Mendi*'s engines and sent Trapnell to find the carpenter, Olsson, and order him to assess the damage below decks. The captain knew the damage to the ship was very serious, however, and ordered the lifeboats to be readied for boarding and gave four blasts on the whistle, the signal for those on board to go to their muster stations by the boats. He asked for the 25-year-old radio operator Harold Mole, but Harold did not come and was never seen again. The first distress signal picked up by the *Brisk* was at 5 am, when the *Darro* sent out an SOS saying that it had been in collision with another vessel.[15] Four minutes later, the *Brisk* radioed the *Mendi* asking whether assistance was required. No reply was received.

Hertslet subsequently remembered being awoken by a 'jolting jar' close to his cabin.[16] Thinking that the ship had run down a fishing boat, he dressed, then heard the signal to go to muster stations. Outside, he saw what he thought was an orderly scene, with men walking or running to their muster stations, and noticed debris in the water. Lieutenant Van Vuren, whose muster station was on the poop deck, remembered a similarly orderly assembly.[17] However, Matli described a chaotic scene in one of the holds as everyone ran and crowded onto the ladder and described being pulled back deliberately before finally making it out of the hatch. Marks Mokwena, a future political activist, also described a less than orderly scene, with men running about in great terror.[18]

On the bridge of the *Brisk*, Lieutenant-Commander Algernon Lyons and his officer of the watch had seen the steaming light of the *Darro* and then, about 15 seconds later, heard the sound of the collision. The time they recorded in the log was 04.57 am.[19] The *Brisk* was not far behind and the helm was put hard to starboard to take them clear before turning back to give assistance.

On the *Mendi*, the gravity of the situation was becoming clear to Captain Yardley and he gave the order to launch the lifeboats. In backing away, the *Darro* had left a huge and very deep hole in the starboard side of the *Mendi* that extended well below the waterline and almost to the keel. One of the survivors from hold 1 subsequently told Captain Hertslet that from where he was lying, he could touch the bow of the *Darro* with one hand and the mainmast of the *Mendi* with the other before the ship backed away.[20] As a result, the sea rushed into hold 1. Even worse, the point of impact was only about 12 feet (3.7m) forward of the watertight bulkhead separating it from hold 2. The force of the impact must have seriously damaged this bulkhead, because hold 2 also started to flood. Had the damage been confined to hold 1, then the *Mendi* might have been able to stay afloat, but with both holds filling rapidly, the ship was doomed.

It is not clear how extensive the immediate casualties were in hold 1. They must have been substantial, although by no means all of the men in hold 1 appear to have been killed by the collision or the subsequent flooding. Vincent Capner, an 18-year-old ordinary seaman from Gloucester, went forward to check that all of the crew were out of their accommodation in the forecastle after his boat had been launched. As he hurried back, he saw men still coming out of one of the hold's booby hatches.

Unfortunately, the flooding was so rapid that the *Mendi* quickly listed heavily to starboard. This meant that the boats on the port side could not be lowered directly into the water and instead made contact with the side of the ship. One of the boats jammed on the deck railing and another was holed when it hit the side of the ship. Although the third was got into the water, when one of the falls was cut to release the trapped foot of 23-year-old Danish lamp trimmer Jens Hangaard, it capsized because it was overloaded. All three boats on the starboard side were launched successfully but, unfortunately, men sliding down the deck because of the list crowded onto no. 5 boat before it could be pulled away, unbalancing and capsizing it. The two boats that did get away could carry only 97 of the more than 800 people on board.

The only option now remaining for those left on board were the life rafts, of which there were 46 – technically enough to accommodate the 920 survivors. Most were stowed on the hatches of the holds fore and aft and, close to the muster points, these rafts were relatively easy to get into the water. Most were launched successfully and one witness from the crew recalled that he saw about 40 in the water. Capner recalled seeing men of the Labour Corps readying the life rafts in a disciplined fashion, although aft Van Vuren recalled that his men struggled to untie the rafts from their stowage lashings in the dark. Matli also remembered men trying to untie the lashings. The fact that they were meant to be cut rather than untied suggests that the men were panicked by then.

The life rafts were primitive by modern standards and were not designed as enclosed dry spaces. More immediately problematic was the fact that the men on deck had to jump into the cold sea in order to reach them. While most of the men were by now wearing their lifebelts and could therefore expect to survive the dangers of cold shock as they hit the water, the prospect of jumping into the dark, freezing sea as the ship sank around them must have been terrifying. Hertslet, who could not swim and recalls having to run back to get his own lifebelt, remembered the order to jump overboard being shouted out and described the frightening decision that he was forced to make:

> And then came the shout from somewhere, 'All overboard! ... boats! ... she's sinking!' For a moment I stood almost paralysed, but gripping the deck-rail. What should I do? ... I couldn't swim, and I had a heavy overcoat on, over which was fastened my lifebelt and I carried a despatch case with chocolate and restoratives in it. There really wasn't much choice ... so I scrambled onto the rail and jumped feet first.[21]

Many other men also struggled to force themselves to jump. In a letter to his family in Durban, 34-year-old Lieutenant Samuel Richardson told them that when some of his men had not followed his lead in jumping in, Richardson reboarded to try to persuade those left to overcome their fears and follow him.[22] It is at some point during the process of abandoning ship that the famous 'death dance' (*see* Chapter 10) is supposed to have occurred.

Within about 20 minutes of the collision, the end came for the *Mendi* and it went down by the bow or 'head'. Matli described how the 'nose' of the ship was already 'deep in the sea' when he jumped onto a life raft that was still tied onto the ship.[23] Matli, who then fell in the water, described how the ship subsequently 'blew three times', possibly the escape or explosion of trapped steam from the boilers, and how he saw two of the crew jump overboard before the ship then sank. Some of the men saw a whirlpool form as the ship sank below the surface, Matli describing it as 'a great hollow'. Captain William Brownlee told how the elderly Lieutenant Samuel Emslie, selected for the SANLC because of his government experience in working with the black population of the Transkei, was torn from their hands and sucked down.[24]

The sinking of the ship left several hundred men either floating in their lifejackets or clinging to the rafts. As his men were preparing the rafts, Van Vuren had glimpsed a large ship through the fog about 200 yards (180m) away,[25] although the subsequent Inquiry concluded that it may have been up to twice that distance away. This was the *Darro*, which was stopped in the water.

The rescue

After the collision, Captain Stump had ordered his carpenter to check the damage to the ship. After backing away from the *Mendi*, he had also ordered his crew to muster at their lifeboat stations and to prepare the lifeboats for launching. No attempt was made to find out what had happened to the vessel that they had collided with, even though a great deal of shouting was heard and even after the first of *Mendi*'s lifeboats, with survivors including Hertslet on board, came alongside about 50 minutes after the collision.

The *Brisk*'s radio log (Fig 8.10) records that an SOS message was received from the ship at 5.40 am, stating that it was sinking. The carpenter had quickly established that the collision bulkhead behind the bow, which was designed to prevent the ship from flooding if the bow was damaged, was intact, and he sent several reports that there was no flooding. Puzzlingly, Stump received the chief officer's report to this effect 10 minutes before the SOS was sent, but it was not until 6.53 am, half an hour after the *Mendi* had sunk, that the *Brisk* radioed ashore to give the following message: 'Steamer *Darro* reports: all O.K. so far'.

In contrast to Stump, the commander of the *Brisk* took immediate action to render assistance. However, his attempts to help were slowed by the fog and the tide, which was now starting to run from east to west. After turning sharply to avoid a further collision, the destroyer turned back and attempted to relocate the *Mendi*. This was not easy. Even though Lieutenant-Commander Lyons was able to get up to the stern of the ship, he was unable to hail it and he described his searchlights as being 'absolutely ineffective' in the fog.[26] Lyons said he saw the *Mendi* moving astern and so took evasive action. The wreck of the ship subsequently came to rest on the seabed with its bow to the west, which suggests that what Lyons saw was that the ship, whose bow had presumably been pushed to port by the force of impact, was turning in the tide, which men in the water later said was starting to run.

As Lyons came back again, he could not see the *Mendi*'s lights, so he stopped the ship close to where shouting could be heard: 'I stopped close to where there was much shouting and sent a whaler with the Sub-Lieutenant to find what assistance might be required, the other boats being manned ready for lowering. The whaler returned at once with men taken from the water and the other boats left immediately.'[27]

The *Brisk*'s search for survivors went on for about four hours after the collision, hampered by the darkness and fog and by the running tide. Trapnell, who was clinging to the upturned hull of the *Mendi*'s capsized No. 5 boat and was rescued after about an hour and a half, told the

Copy.	Receiving Ship.	Transmitting Ship.	Time of Despatch or Receipt.	Tune.	Remarks.	Message.
			Date... 21st February 1917.			H.M.S. "BRISK"
	All ships, s.s.Mendi	s.s.Darro	5.0 am 5.4 am	qq	En clair(P.method) no answer	S.O.S. s.s. Darro in collision ten miles South of St. Catherine's. Is there any assistance required, can you proceed and at what speed ?
	s.s.Darro	"	5.33 am	qqq	En clair	What is extent of damage ?
	All ships	s.s.Darro	5.38 am		En clair	Will find out.
	C-in-C's Plymouth Portsmth	s.s.Darro	5.40 am	q	En clair	S.O.S. s.s. Darro sinking twelve South of St. Catherines. 0520. Convoy Mendi in collision, damage unknown.
	Brisk	Brisk	5.42 a.m.	q	Vocabulary via Niton SS/6.58 (local interference)	
	Brisk	Brisk	6.8 a.m.	q	Vocabulary via Niton 6.19 am	0600. Mendi sunk picking up survivors. Darro reports sinking.
	Brisk Darro Brisk	Brisk Darro Brisk	6.23 am. 6.26 am. 6.44 am.	qqq	En clair En clair Commercial - made several times - no reply	Do you want any assistance ? How are you getting on ? All O.K. so far. Have you anything to communicate ?
	Brisk	Brisk	6.53 am	q.	Vocabulary via Niton at 7.1 am	0645 Steamer Darro reports: all O.K. so far.
	Capt.D II Brisk s.s.Darro	Capt.D II Brisk	7.8 am 7.23 am	qq	Vocabulary Commercial - several calls - no reply	0655 Indicate Mendi's position at time of sinking. Have you anything to communicate?
	Brisk	Brisk	7.33 am	q	Vocabulary via Niton /34	0730 Reply 0655. 10 miles South of St.Catherine's. Captain of MENDI onboard.
	Brisk s.s.Darro Brisk Brisk	ss. Darro s.s.Darro s.s.Darro s.s.Darro	7.45 am 7.49 am 7.51 am 8.34 am	qqqqq	En clair En clair En clair General Service	O.K. here up to present. What is the extent of damage ? Still awaiting instructions from bridge. I have sent to bridge for instructions. DARRO collided with MENDI 8 miles South of St. Catherine's Point. Trying to make Southampton fog preventing it will shortly proceed to port.
	s.s. Darro Capt.D II S.O.Portsmth Defences.	Brisk Brisk Brisk Morlot	8.55 am 9.13 am 9.18 am 9.22 am	qqqq	General Service Vocabulary Vocabulary Vocabulary	If s.s. Southampton fog preventing I still require and BRISK proceed. 0820 Do not require and BRISK proceed ? What is your magnetic curse and speed ? When did you leave scene of collision ? 0820 Have picked up DARRO escorting her to St. Helens at slow speed.
	Brisk Brisk C-in-C Portsmth Defences Capt.D II	ss. Darro Capt.D II	10.12 am 10.42 am.	qq	General Service. Vocabulary	North East dead slow just leaving scene. 0940 Your 0910. To the most convenient defended port. After, returning to base.
	C-in-C S.O.Portsmth Defences	Brisk	10.50 am	q	Vocabulary	1030 Am proceeding to St.Helens Roads with survivors of MENDI. Captain, 4 officers, 11 white ratings, 1 military officer, 3 sergeants, many coloured men saved.
	Brisk	Brisk	11.16 am	q	Vocabulary	1100 Weather permitting expect arrive 12.45 pm. 70 natives saved, 10 dead on board.
	Capt.D II	Capt.D II	11.40 am	q	Vocabulary	1106 Report what base you are proceeding to utilise local patrol boats for landing survivors if possible.
	Capt D II	Brisk	12.5 pm	q	Vocabulary	1200 Proceeding to St. Helens arrive at 1 p.m.

Fig 8.10 Radio log of the Brisk. *[© The National Archives MT9/115]*

subsequent Inquiry that the *Brisk*'s boats had arrived: 'Almost as soon as the accident happened but it was thick (very foggy) at the time, it was impossible to find us; there were voices all round us calling out for help; it was impossible to be everywhere at once.'[28]

Another vessel, the tramp steamer *Sandsend* arrived to help, possibly alerted by the *Darro*'s SOS. Its boats picked up a total of 23 survivors, including Matli, who quickly recovered from his ordeal enough to complain that the cocoa he was given was only lukewarm.[29]

The *Darro* remained on the scene until 10.12 am, when it radioed the *Brisk* to say that it was leaving the scene. In all that time, nothing had been done by the crew of the *Darro* to help the survivors in the water, and the boats that did reach the ship were abandoned and left to drift away instead of being sent back to help. It proceeded under escort to the St Helen's Road anchorage off the east coast of the Isle of Wight. From there it went into Portsmouth, where it landed 107 survivors. The *Sandsend* transferred its 23 survivors to the minesweeper *Balfour* and they were landed in Newhaven.

The *Brisk* left the scene at 10.30 am.[30] Catching up with the *Darro*, Lyons eventually landed 137 survivors, including Captain Yardley and other men of the crew. A raft with a few survivors on board subsequently managed to reach the Dorset coast. The last to be picked up may have been Ndbele Alpheus Moliwa Zagubi and his two companions. Zagubi's family said that they drifted for two or three days before being picked up, a remarkable feat of survival given the cold.[31]

Altogether there were only 267 survivors, less than one-third of those who had left Plymouth. Mtolo, Tshite, MacTavish, Richardson, Raine, Carroll and Mole were not among them. Joseph Tshite died as he tried to encourage those in the water around him by singing hymns and saying prayers.[32] Some of the dead were recovered, but most had to be left in the water by the exhausted rescuers.

9

Aftermath and inquiry

The living and the dead

The survivors were taken to hospitals and camps before being sent on to France. Hertslet hobbled into a hospital and spent five days there being treated for thrombosis. When released, he went to stay in the London house of one of the men who had left the ship at Plymouth, which had been converted into a nursing home for officers. From there he went on to France, where he was posted to work at No. 1 Hospital in Le Havre.[1]

Matli recalled that, after doing kitchen duties on his rescue ship, he was first taken to a guest house and then to a military camp, which he shared with a contingent of the SANLC who had sailed on the *Kenilworth Castle* and Captain McLean of his own unit, who had been put ashore at Plymouth with appendicitis. Having at first been told that he was going home, McLean was sent to France two weeks later. During the cross-channel voyage, the crew pointed out the site of the disaster to him.[2]

Although the precise figures are still in doubt, 646 men were officially recorded to have been lost. Of these, two were military officers, seven non-commissioned officers, 607 were labourers and 30 were crew members. An additional member of the crew, the 28-year-old assistant steward L J Adams, died of pneumonia during the voyage.

Those recovered dead from the water and those who died after rescue were taken ashore and buried. Several men were buried in Milton Cemetery in Portsmouth, including Sergeant MacTavish (Fig 9.1). His black comrades were treated as unequally in death as they were in life and had to share plots. MacTavish, who was white, had his own.

In the days and weeks that followed the disaster, bodies were washed up along the south coast of England and in France. Inquests were quickly held and the bodies were buried in churchyards near to where they came ashore. Drifting in the tide, some passed through the Strait of Dover and ended up on Dutch beaches. The body of Sikaniso Mtolo was one such, washed up at Zandvoort a couple of months later. The Public Prosecutor at Haarlem issued the following certificate.

The Public Prosecutor in Haarlem
Declares to have no objections against the burial of the body of a male,
presumably (a black man) and named Sikanisu Mtolo, age about 40 years
whose body was washed ashore in Zandvoort from/out of the North Sea on
29 April 1917, whose cause of death may be assumed was drowning

Haarlem, 30 April 1917
The Public Prosecutor in Haarlem[3]

*Fig 9.1 Sergeant
MacTavish's grave, with the
original wooden cross.
[MacTavish Family Archives]*

Mtolo was identified because his identity certificate was found with his
body, folded up tightly in a pocket. Initially buried in Zandvoort in 1920,
he was moved to the Commonwealth cemetery at Noordwijk, where he is
buried in a single plot with three black comrades from the *Mendi* (Fig 9.2).
The cemetery contains many victims of the war at sea, including some
of the dead from the cruisers *Aboukir*, *Cressy* and *Hogue*, which were
torpedoed in a calamitous incident early in the war.

Most of the dead, however, were never found, their bodies having
disappeared without trace. Their names are listed on the Hollybrook
Memorial in Southampton, along with those of nearly 1,900 land and
airforce servicemen and women of the Commonwealth whose graves are

*Fig 9.2 The grave of Privates
Sikaniso Mtolo, Arosi Zenzile,
Sitebe Molide and Natal Kazimula
at Noordwijk. [© Mark Sijlmans]*

unknown – men and women whose bodies were lost at sea or otherwise
unrecovered. Many were lost in troop transports or other vessels that were
mined or torpedoed in home waters. Almost one-third of the names are of
victims of the *Mendi* disaster.[4]

News reaches South Africa

News of the disaster reached the South African Government in a telegram
on 24 February, but the names of those saved and those presumed dead
were not confirmed until 7 March 1917.

The official announcement was made by Prime Minister General Botha
to the House of Assembly on 9 March, more than two weeks after the
sinking.[5] In the meantime, rumour and distrust were rife among the native
population, many of whom were already aware of the disaster: some of the
surviving officers appear to have telegraphed news of their survival home.
Botha apologised to members of the House of Assembly for the delay in
making a public announcement.

A telegram was sent to magistrates throughout the country, who called
meetings with chiefs and headmen to read the telegram and answer
questions. Memorial services, accompanied by an outpouring of deep
and dignified sorrow, were held across South Africa, with huge numbers
attending.

Bertha, the wife of Sergeant MacTavish, was informed of the death of her husband by a letter dated 24 February.[6] Because of opposition by the South African Government, South African members of the SANLC did not receive the British War Medals that the British Government had awarded to all those who served in the war. However, Mrs MacTavish did subsequently receive two printed scrolls (Fig 9.3), one of which was signed by King George V and stated:

> I join with my grateful people in sending you this memorial of a brave life given for others in the Great War[7]

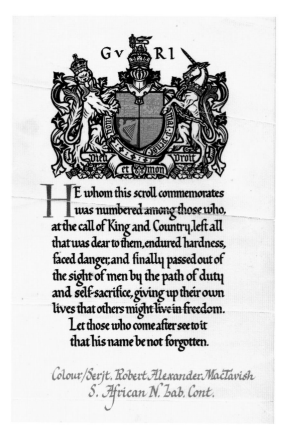

Fig 9.3 Commemorative scroll received by the widow of Sergeant MacTavish in 1921. These were issued after the war to the next of kin of service personnel who died, along with a bronze Memorial Plaque. This medallion, more than one million of which were issued, was nicknamed the 'Widow's Penny' or 'Dead Man's Penny'. [MacTavish Family Archives]

The death of Sikaniso Mtolo seems to have hit his family very hard. His grandchildren recall that things became difficult and his wife Thoko moved back from Mtolo's kraal to her own family. Later, Mtolo's family abandoned the kraal and today it lies under a forestry plantation.[8]

The inquiry

The five-day Board of Trade Court of Inquiry into the loss of the *Mendi* was held in Caxton Hall in London in late July and early August 1917. Due to the sensitivity of the tragedy, it had been hoped to appoint a magistrate to conduct the investigation who was experienced in conducting Board of Trade inquiries. However, as none were available, the presiding magistrate, J G Hay Halkett, was assisted by three captains and commanders in the Royal Navy and Royal Naval Reserve.

Formal inquiries of this type in wartime were unusual and reflected British concern to demonstrate to the South African Government that the disaster was being properly investigated. Both the Board of Trade and the South African Government were represented. News of the disaster had not been covered up and there was sufficient public interest for each day's evidence to be covered in the national newspapers.

The Court of Inquiry heard from 18 witnesses, principally the two captains and other members of their crews. It proved difficult to secure the presence of the SANLC and naval officers because of wartime demands and therefore their evidence was given by affidavit or report. The Inquiry also heard from expert witnesses, and the naval architect and surveyor George Brace gave evidence that the ship would probably not have sunk had the flooding been confined to hold 1. There does not appear to have been any attempt to hear from the black members of the SANLC.

As well as establishing the basic facts, the Court was concerned to establish what had caused the loss of life and damage. Appreciating the great sensitivity of this issue, considerable effort had been and was being made by the Board of Trade Maritime Department to reassure both the Court and the South African Government that the *Mendi* had been carrying sufficient lifesaving equipment. While it was admitted in correspondence with the Admiralty and the South Africans that regulations would have required the ship to carry more lifeboats and fewer life rafts had it sailed from a British port,[9] in the event the Court declared itself satisfied with the equipment that had been provided. It blamed the loss of life not on a lack of boats but on the rapid listing of the ship and on the abnormal coldness of the water, which it said made the life rafts less effective than would otherwise have been the case.

The Court also sought to establish whether either captain was at fault and it had the power to suspend or cancel their certificates if it believed that they were to blame. After hearing the evidence, they exonerated Yardley. However, despite the fact that the other seafarers present proved reluctant to blame him, the Court found against Stump. They held that the *Darro* had been going too fast and had not been navigated 'with proper and seamanlike care'.[10] They found that he had breached his responsibilities under British law to render assistance to the *Mendi* and that he had caused loss of life and damage to both ships. In its judgement, the Court stated that his inaction was 'inexcusable'.

It is not hard to sense a strong undercurrent of suppressed outrage on the part of those examining Stump and his officers. Nevertheless, the Court decided that Stump's punishment should be the suspension of his master's certificate for the period of only 12 months, rather than its cancellation, which others appear to have expected. Although the punishment meted out does appear remarkably light given the scale of the loss of life, it was wartime, and Britain was in the middle of an increasingly desperate fight to keep its maritime supply lines open. Highly experienced merchant ship captains were in short supply.

The villain?

Henry Winchester Stump was born in London in 1866, the son of an artificial-limb maker and the grandson of a noted miniature painter. Rather than following in his father's footsteps, Stump went to sea. Having passed his exams and been awarded his 'Certificate of Competency as Master of a Foreign-Going Ship' in October 1896 at the age of 30,[11] he was employed between 1896 and 1905 as Third, Second and finally First Mate, before commanding his first ship as Master in 1906.[12] Stump resumed command in 1919 after his suspension and commanded a further 14 vessels before his retirement in 1931.

The punishment meted out to Stump for his role in the loss of the *Mendi* seems to have been regarded by many as too lenient. A faction within the Board of Trade certainly thought so, and a barrister's opinion was sought as to whether he could be subject to a successful criminal prosecution for his failure to render assistance. In the event, Eminent Counsel Sir Reginald Ackland thought not and the matter was reluctantly dropped. Captain A H Young probably spoke for many of his colleagues when he responded to this advice. In a note handwritten on official minutes, he said that he considered that what Stump had done was 'one of the gravest instances on record' of a failure to assist. He went on to express the opinion that he was unfit for command and angrily wrote that he 'should forever be precluded from the command of a Brit[ish] ship. Such a man is a standing menace to seafarers'.[13]

But was Young right to think this of Stump? Was he really a menace? As a master, Stump was no stranger to serious accidents. On 23 August 1916, when in command of the *Darro's* sister vessel, the *Drina*, and outbound from Liverpool to Lisbon with coal and general cargo, he collided with a topsail schooner off Carnarvon Lighthouse. That collision also occurred at night and in dense fog. Although he was not new to the *Darro* and had commanded it in 1916, the day before the *Mendi* disaster occurred, Stump struck the quay wall in Le Havre while manoeuvring. In 1921, he also collided with and sank a trawler while in command of the *Cisneros*. It is not known whether, or to what extent, Stump was to blame for any of these collisions, however, and there is no record of proceedings being taken against him after any of them.

At the Inquiry, Stump was questioned at length about why he had driven his ship at full speed through the fog and why he had not used sound signals as required by law. He came across as evasive and contradicted himself. He told the Court that he was worried about alerting enemy submarines by blowing his whistle and that he had received instructions about maintaining speed and silence. However, he was unable to provide any details about who had given him these instructions, and the Court clearly did not believe him. He also said that he had been told by the French authorities to make sure that he had reached the English coast by daylight and that this justified his speed and his silence. The Court disagreed. Furthermore, he said that he had not expected a troopship to be there, an excuse that appears to have been regarded as particularly unconvincing, given the very large number of vessels moving along and across the Channel every day.

With regard to why he had not taken any steps to render assistance, Stump offered up a range of excuses that were either weak or were contradicted by others, including men from his own crew. He had been steaming at full speed, so must have known that the collision was likely to have caused catastrophic damage to the vessel he had run into. He told the Court that he thought that his own vessel was in danger, but it was clear that he knew, or should have known very quickly, that it was not. It was not therefore necessary to hold his own boats back for emergency use (he had 24 at his disposal), and his claim that to have used them in the fog would have put them at risk was not treated seriously. He claimed not to have enough men to man both the boats and the ship, yet his crew numbered 163. His claims that he could not hear, or that he had misunderstood, the cries of the men in the water were contradicted by witnesses from his own crew, who told the Court that such cries could be heard for several hours. The Court noted that even when two boatloads and a raft of survivors had come alongside, he made no enquiries and took no action.

There is little doubt that Stump had little awareness or concern for the risk his speed posed to vessels like the *Mendi*, but it is possible to find some reason behind the recklessness. The threat of U-boats was very real, and it is possible that this drove him to run what he thought, perhaps with some degree of justification, was a small risk of actually running into another ship. However, if he feared that threat so much, it is difficult to understand why he kept his ship at the scene of the disaster for several hours.

With regard to his failure to render assistance, this remains unexplained and perhaps unexplainable. It is hard to find any credible mitigation. And yet Stump received a character reference from his employers and continued to work as a master when his suspension was over. His crew and others who gave evidence do not appear to have expressed any critical opinions about him in their evidence,[14] although it is true that it would have taken a brave seaman to directly criticise an experienced captain.

Although the Chief Officer of the *Darro*, Henry Womersley, gave evidence to the Inquiry that nobody in the *Mendi*'s boats mentioned other survivors, he admitted that he did not ask them any questions.[15] Hertslet's affidavit states that he had spoken to Stump after he had reached the *Darro* and was told by him that he had thought he had run into a tramp and that the men in the boats were the entire crew.

Womersley's evidence went in defence of his captain, but the reported dialogue between him and the examining magistrate and his assistants suggests that they remained highly sceptical. Second Officer Edwards said he thought that the cries that were heard came from the men in the boats rather than from men in the water, but it is clear from the evidence given by the ordinary seamen on board the *Darro* that cries for help went on long after the men in the boats had been rescued. Ernest Milford claimed that they could plainly be heard all round the ship for at least two hours, and another seaman, Henry Cotter, said that some of the deck crew wanted to go to their assistance.[16]

Hertslet's son said his father told him that Stump was drunk.[17] While alcoholism was certainly not unheard of among merchant seamen, this was presumably said to him only much later and is not mentioned in other accounts.

Captain Young of the Board of Trade may have got to the truth of the matter in his response to Counsel's opinion when he said, 'Either the master was utterly callous to all sentiments of humanity or, as a result of the collision, his nerve deserted him to such an extent as to render him incapable of rational thought and action.'[18]

The weight of evidence, or perhaps more accurately the lack of it, seems to suggest that once the *Darro* had pulled away from the *Mendi*, Stump's powers of decision-making deserted him. Although it would appear that he must have known his ship was safe very quickly, he failed to adapt his response accordingly. He then failed to do anything to help the vessel he had struck, even though there was nothing apparently stopping him from doing so, and even after Hertslet boarded his ship and confronted him. Perhaps personal fear of enemy submarines, his desire to protect his own ship, a concern for the consequences upon his own career or the apparently poor communication on board swayed his decision.[19] Perhaps he was hampered by a lack of information from his officers, but he had more than enough time to rectify this himself.

When asked at the Inquiry why he had left the scene of the disaster at slow speed when he had claimed to have received instructions about maintaining speed, Stump said 'I had got into enough trouble already'. This does not sound like the response of a man entirely devoid of a conscience, but for whom was he concerned – the men who had died or merely himself? For the present time, Stump remains an enigma.

Compensation claims

Following the Inquiry, the claims against the owners of the *Darro*, the Royal Mail Steam Packet Company Limited, brought a 'limited liability' action in the High Court. At the time, maritime law entitled it to ask the court what the maximum total amount was that it could be held liable to pay to all potential claimants. Using the calculation based on tonnage prevailing at the time, the court decided that its liability would be limited to £163,904.14s.0d: £87,415.16.10d for the ship and contents and £76,488.17s.2d for death and injury.[20]

Surviving relatives had to pursue claims against the owners of the *Darro* if they then wanted to secure compensation from this fund. Sergeant MacTavish's widow, Annie, received a telegram advising her that the South African High Commissioner in London had established that non-commissioned officers were entitled to £300. Annie, who was also entitled to a pension, accepted.

The families of the dead men of the SANLC who were not officers were less generously provided for. The British Government gave them a standard payment of £50 and very few would have been entitled to any form of pension.[21]

Twenty-eight-year-old Second Officer Herbert Raine, who had originally gone to sea in 1905, was rescued from the sea but died of exposure shortly afterwards. His inquest was held in Portsmouth in February, when a verdict of accidental death was reached. His mother, Ellen, brought dependency claims against the owners of the *Darro*: £500 for herself; £125 for his 20-year-old sister Beatrice, who was in delicate health and did not work; plus £85.5s for lost effects.[22] A dependency claim was also brought by the housekeeper mother of 16-year-old deck boy William Foster. She and her nine-year-old daughter appear to have been awarded £152.[23]

Why did so many die?

While the scale of the loss of life caused by the sinking of the *Mendi* was by no means unique during the war, it is clear from the reaction when news emerged that it was exceptional. Indeed it remains to this day one of the worst disasters at sea to befall South Africa.

It was therefore inevitable that the Board of Trade Inquiry into the loss should consider why so many died. It asked the following questions:

- Were the life-saving appliances on board the SS *Mendi* adequate and proper in the circumstances?
- Were proper steps taken to instruct those on board in the use of such appliances in case of need?
- Were proper steps taken after the collision to make effective use of such appliances?

The Inquiry concluded that the *Mendi* was adequately equipped with lifesaving equipment 'in the circumstances' and that had the water been warmer, a much larger proportion of the men on board would have been saved.

It also heard from witnesses that lifeboat and life-raft drills supervised by the officers and crew had been carried out regularly, and, indeed, that during the last nine or ten days of the voyage, such drills had been performed daily, with the entire crew and battalion mustering at the boats and rafts and putting on their lifebelts. The Inquiry concluded from the evidence that it heard that almost all the life rafts had been launched and that the great majority of men rescued or seen in the water had been wearing their lifebelts.

The Inquiry concluded that men had been killed as a direct result of the collision, but, while this is almost certainly true, the exact number of such losses is unknown. The *Darro* had driven very deeply into the side of hold 1, causing catastrophic damage. The temporary wooden decks on the starboard side may well have collapsed, falling onto the men below and throwing lethal debris across the hold. It is unknown how many of the men who were trying to sleep in there were killed by the impact, but it is probable that there were many, and even more are likely to have been killed by the massive inrush of water as the *Darro* disengaged itself and pulled away. What happened in the depths of hold 2 also remains a mystery, but the failure of the bulkhead that separated it from the impact and the speed of sinking suggest that it flooded rapidly and that men may have been killed there. Those in hold 1 that survived the impact and the flood of water that followed – most likely those above the waterline and on the port side – would have had to struggle in the dark, probably over debris and perhaps over their comrades, to try to reach the ladder that led up to a single hatch. To make matters worse, the hatch lay on the same side of the ship as the impact. Lieutenant van Vuren swore an affidavit that the men who had been sleeping on the temporary decks in hold 1 did not muster at their boat stations, and he thought that the doors of the small 'booby hatch' used to get in and out of the hold without taking the main hatch cover off had jammed shut, preventing their escape.[24] However, one of the surviving crew, Vincent Capner, told the Inquiry that he had seen men climbing out of this hatch. The Inquiry therefore concluded that the men who had failed to appear had probably been killed by the initial collision or drowned by the inrush of water that followed.

Lifesaving equipment

The Inquiry does not mention the concerns expressed at the time, both within and outside government circles, about the number of lifeboats carried by the ship. The *Mendi* had six wooden lifeboats of different sizes, as well as a gig – a ship's boat that could be used as a makeshift lifeboat. The boats were carried on either side of the upper deck and all except the gig were already swung out on davits, ready for launch (Fig 9.4). This was achieved by lowering them by block and tackle down into the water. Unlike a modern lifeboat, they were not enclosed, so they were vulnerable to flooding and those in them took the full force of the weather. Fortunately, the sea was calm when the ship sank and anyone who managed to get into one of these boats could have expected to survive the disaster.

There were, however, still two problems with the *Mendi's* lifeboats that undoubtedly contributed to the scale of the tragedy that befell the ship. First, they could safely carry only 298 people, in other words far fewer than the number of men actually on board. Inevitably, most of the men on board would have to jump into the freezing water and suffer the consequences. Although the Board of Trade had been anxious to assure the Inquiry that there had been enough lifeboats, it did admit in correspondence that the provision of lifesaving equipment depended upon where the ship sailed from. Second, because the *Mendi* developed a heavy list to starboard very soon after the collision, lowering of the lifeboats on the port side was

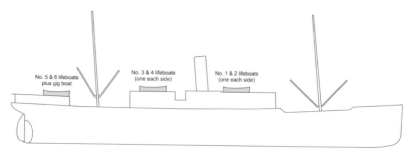

Fig 9.4 Location of the Mendi's *lifeboats. [© Wessex Archaeology]*

obstructed by the side of the ship. As a result, only two of the six dedicated lifeboats were successfully launched.

The great majority of the men left on board had no alternative other than to jump into the sea with the men who had already been spilled into the water from lifeboats or to wait for the water to rise to them as the ship sank. Lieutenant van Vuren told the Inquiry that after the loss of the two lifeboats under his charge, he ordered the life rafts to be lowered. Realising that the ship would soon sink, and thinking that they would be picked up quickly, van Vuren ordered his three platoons to jump overboard about 15 minutes after the collision occurred.

No evidence appears to exist to suggest that the men had any means of climbing down the side of the ship, such as scrambling nets. Although Captain Yardley was able to walk into the water as the bridge submerged and some men may have jumped directly into the rafts, most probably jumped into the water. Their chances of surviving this and getting to a raft would therefore have depended heavily upon whether or not they were wearing one of the ship's lifebelts. The ship is recorded as having carried more than a thousand lifebelts, including 160 in the accommodation, 100 in two boxes on the navigating bridge and 810 in bales of 40 and 50 in the troop accommodation in the holds. It appears likely that each man had his lifebelt to hand (Fig 9.5).

Simple inflatable lifebelts had been introduced prior to the start of the war, but those carried by the *Mendi* instead relied upon the buoyancy of cork. Such lifebelts had been in existence since the late 18th century, and by the mid-19th century, there were many designs. A typical troopship lifebelt consisted of cork or kapok pieces sewn onto a canvas belt, tied around the upper body and with adjustable shoulder straps. The *Mendi's* lifebelts were probably like this as they are described as being 'the usual "tie on" pattern' in a Board of Trade letter written in June 1917[25] and as 'ordinary cork pattern' at the Inquiry. When fitted properly, this type of lifebelt could float an unconscious survivor face up, but although it would

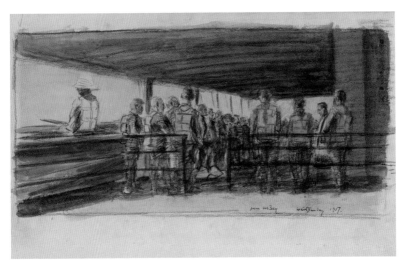

Fig 9.5 *Watercolour by James McBey showing a group of British sailors and soldiers taking service on the deck of a troopship in 1917. The men are shown wearing lifejackets.*
[© Imperial War Museum ART 1405]

still provide buoyancy if fitted too low, around the waist, if the wearer lost consciousness, he would probably float face down and drown.

Many witnesses describe either wearing lifebelts themselves or having seen other men wearing them. Jacob Matli reminisced that 'Everybody was having his lifebelt on and in full kit'.[26] In 1918, Marks Mokwena recalled that he heard the shout go up to 'Put on your lifebelts and you will all be saved'.[27] Van Vuren told the Inquiry that once the men were in the water, 'some like myself were kept up by their lifebelts'. William Mathumetse, who was just 16 years of age, saw two dead men floating in their lifebelts. Captain Yardley, who was wearing his lifebelt when he walked into the water as it rose to the bridge of the sinking ship, told the Inquiry that he noticed, once he was in the water, that all of the men he saw around him had lifebelts on.

While it seems likely from these accounts that the majority of men were wearing lifebelts, the experience of Captain Hertslet suggests that this was not universally the case. He initially left his lifebelt in his cabin and it was only after looking around the deck and the smoking room that he risked going back for it. In the end, this proved a wise decision: when he entered the water wearing a heavy overcoat, it was only his life belt that saved him. He described the experience as follows: 'Pheuf! The water was cold! Eight degrees above freezing they told us afterwards. I remember going under, wondering if I'd ever come up again, but the belt held me up, and then I took two or three spasmodic, floundering and despairing strokes and got to the side of the boat.'[28]

Hertslet was lucky: he managed to get to a raft and get onto it before his strength ebbed away completely. Any of the men who jumped off the *Mendi* who were not wearing a lifebelt were in a far worse position. They are much less likely to have been able to get into a raft and are likely to have drowned very quickly. Even those who reached the relative safety of the life rafts were far from being saved, however.

The *Mendi* was fitted with 46 rafts provided by the Admiralty, which were stowed on the hatches in the well decks, about 20 aft and the remainder forward. They are reported to have been 'buoyant air tank type, each fitted with lifelines round the structure, and each capable of supporting about 20 persons in the water', and Yardley told the Inquiry that they could be easily handled by two men.[29] A photograph taken by Lieutenant Powell on board the *Mendi* while it was sailing to East Africa shows stacks of liferafts on the boat deck (*see* Fig 8.2). These rafts are what today might be called 'floats', constructed out of wooden slats with lifelines attached to the sides. Rectangular and a little bit longer than an average man, the wooden structure encased one or more air tanks, which theoretically kept the small flat deck space the raft provided just above the water. The raft was reversible, so that it would always float 'right way up' when thrown into the sea. Although theoretically able to accommodate 20 people, however, there was only enough space on the raft for 6 men to sit on each, the remainder having to cling onto a lifeline. As the raft was not enclosed, it could not keep those on the deck very dry, and in anything other than a smooth sea, it would have been very unstable for those sitting on it.

Ordinary Seaman Vincent Capner told the Inquiry that he saw men of the Labour Corps on the forward well deck getting the rafts out in an orderly fashion under the direction of their officers, though other evidence suggests that there was some difficulty. Yardley told the Inquiry that the rafts, which could be lifted easily by two men, were tied down using signal halyards or rope yarn and seems to have assumed that these would be cut when the rafts were needed. It had been agreed between Yardley and the SANLC officers that they would be responsible for launching the rafts when needed,[30] but it is not clear that they knew exactly what to do. Van Vuren recalled that in the darkness his men struggled to untie the ropes securing the rafts, and not all of them could be launched over the side. Nevertheless, it appears likely that most were launched, and Quartermaster Thomas told the Inquiry that he thought that he had seen about 40 of them in the water. It is not known whether these rafts were tied to the *Mendi* while the men jumped in or whether they were allowed to float free, but the fact that so many were seen suggests that they did not immediately drift off when lowered into the water.

It is possible that the *Mendi* also carried Carley floats (Fig 9.6).[31] These had an O-shaped copper tube covered in buoyant kapok or cork and sealed by canvas, with lifelines around the outside. Like other life rafts of the period, they were designed to be reversible and, instead of a solid floor, had a grating, which let water through. Anyone jumping into the sea would be expected to swim to a float and either hang off the side or, if there was room, climb onto the ring.

Regardless of whether they were wooden floats or Carleys, however, almost all life rafts of the time had one major shortcoming: most of those they were designed to save would have had to stay in the water and even those on top of the rafts would still have been in or very close to the water. As a result, all of the occupants were extremely vulnerable to hypothermia. Those hanging onto the lifelines were also in grave danger from the shorter-term and disabling effects of superficial nerve and skin cooling. An inquiry into the performance of Carleys in the Second World War noted that 'Time and again large numbers who have reached their refuge (the raft) have collapsed from cramp and cold and died before rescue arrived'.[32]

Fig 9.6 A Carley float in action, 1945. [© Imperial War Museum A30732]

The problem of cold shock and hypothermia

The spasmodic, floundering strokes that Hertslet described himself having taken when he landed in the water are the classic signs of cold shock experienced by anyone jumping or falling into cold water from a sinking vessel. It is caused by sudden skin cooling, which in turn over-stimulates thermoreceptor nerve endings. The colder the water is, the stronger the cold shock experienced.

Although water temperatures off the Isle of Wight in February are commonly 7 degrees centigrade or less, it may have been much colder that February than Hertslet remembered. The winter of 1916–19 was notoriously cold and led to much suffering among the soldiers in the trenches of the Western Front. Surface sea temperatures for various recording locations in the English Channel suggest that the February mean was significantly lower than normal, and the mean temperature recorded at the Owers Light Vessel off Selsey Bill to the east of the wreck site was only 4.5 degrees.[33] At the Inquiry following the sinking, it was recorded that the water temperature was 'about 38 degrees Fahrenheit' (3.3 degrees centigrade).

Cold shock makes it much more difficult to breath-hold and can cause severe breathing difficulties, progressing from gasping to hyperventilation, which can even result in drowning. It can also cause cardiac arrest if the person has an underlying heart condition. Cold shock lasts for only about two minutes but it is followed by a period of about 30 minutes in which the legs and arms cool rapidly and lose strength and coordination ebbs away. After about 15 minutes in very cold water, it usually becomes impossible for a victim to climb onto a raft and very difficult for them to hang onto a lifeline. Psychological preparation and previous exposure to a coldwater environment can help, but eventually, anyone who is not wearing a lifebelt, and who is therefore unable to keep their head above the water, will drown.

Deep body cooling or hypothermia is a major killer of those who have to abandon ship. The human body loses heat through convection in cold water about 25 times more quickly than it does in air. Normal body temperature is about 37 degrees centigrade. As core temperature drops, confusion and disorientation set in and motor skills, including the ability to swim, diminish. Once the body temperature drops to about 30 degrees centigrade, a casualty will become unconsciousness, which means, too, that if the head of the casualty is not being supported out of the water, drowning is likely to occur. Assuming the casualty avoids drowning, their core temperature will continue to cool until it reaches about 28 degrees centigrade, at which point cardiac arrest can occur.

The rate of cooling depends upon a number of factors. Heat is lost from the body in proportion to its surface area and body fat is an excellent insulator, so larger, more heavily built people cool more slowly than do small, thin people. Clothing that insulates the body by trapping air against the skin also slows cooling. Conversely, physical exertion increases heat loss, so a casualty who is wearing a lifebelt, and therefore does not have to swim, will normally survive longer.

Nevertheless, anyone who can stay afloat can survive longer in very cold water than is commonly perceived. In water at 10 degrees centigrade, it could be an hour and a half or more before serious symptoms occur and, depending upon the rate of cooling, it is possible for a casualty to survive more than five hours. In water at 5 degrees centigrade, the survival time drops, but is nevertheless likely to be between one and three hours.

Most of the men who managed to reach the rafts would have been unable to climb onto them – either because of lack of space or because the cold water had drained away the physical strength and coordination they needed to do so – and would have instead hung onto the lifelines. Van Vuren was helped onto the raft that he had reached but Hertslet was not so lucky and described how he was unable to climb into the lifeboat that he managed to reach and was forced to hold onto the side. He described what happened on the rafts around him: 'Some of my men were on rafts some like myself were kept up by their life belts. The water was bitterly cold and I saw some of the natives collapsing of cold but the great majority kept swimming for a long time.' Hertslet described the experience of hanging onto the side of a lifeboat as follows: 'It was intensely cold ... and very soon I couldn't feel my legs at all ... and after a bit my arms began to get paralysed and numb. After what seemed to be hours, but was probably less than half an hour I couldn't hold on any longer.'

Both of these accounts suggest that the men who they observed to die succumbed at least in part to the effects of superficial nerve and skin cooling. Hertslet was fortunate that the men sitting in the lifeboat he was hanging onto responded to his cries for help and dragged him into the boat, where he lay in a heap. When the boat came alongside the *Darro* about 50 minutes after the collision, a number of exhausted men were still hanging onto the lifelines and they and Hertslet had to be carried onto the ship.

Having been struck and briefly stunned by part of the foremast as the ship sank, Captain Yardley managed to reach a raft, which he told the Inquiry was occupied by between 14 and 16 men of the Labour Corps. While he hung onto a lifeline, he recalled that one of the men on it died of exposure and others 'expired' from the cold as the raft was being towed to safety by one of HMS *Brisk*'s boats. Yardley himself seems to have been almost unconscious by the time he reached the warship and was pulled out of the water. (It would, of course, have been an exhausting business hauling men in heavy sodden clothing into the rescue boats.)

As well as being harder to find, men such as William Mathumetse who did not manage to reach a life raft immediately were especially vulnerable, because the effort of swimming around looking for help led to rapid cooling. Mathumetse recalled being unable to recite the Lord's Prayer in the right order. The fact that he survived the effects of cooling to tell his story is probably at least partly down to the fact that he found two dead men in lifebelts who he was able to float on, minimising the proportion of his body in contact with the water.

These recollections and others suggest that most of the men in the water died because they succumbed to hypothermia before they were found and rescued. Captain Yardley said to the Inquiry that 'there were hundreds of boys around me after the wreck. They died from exposure.'

According to an account written by an SANLC officer and published in the same year in the South African *Christian Express* periodical, a white sergeant who had been in the water for a long time was saved heroically by his men and was dragged into a raft where attempts were made to keep him warm. Although he lost consciousness and the raft was not picked up until it had drifted well out into the Channel, he survived the experience.[34]

Witnesses described 'a great hollow' that sucked men down with the ship. Lieutenant Emslie is thought to have been lost in this way and Second Officer Raine and the lamp trimmer Hougaard were dragged down into the water from the upturned keel of No. 4 boat before managing to surface. Both were picked up by the *Brisk*. Hougaard was unconscious, presumably as a result of hypothermia, but survived. Raine had a broken leg and died on the *Brisk*.[35]

All of the witnesses seem to be agreed that the *Mendi* took about 20 to 25 minutes to sink. Men seem to have been ordered to start jumping overboard after about 15 minutes. No boats were launched by the *Darro* to help and although the *Brisk* was able to begin searching for survivors very quickly, the rescue was slowed by the difficulty of spotting men and rafts in the water in the dark and the thick fog and by the current that witnesses noted was running. None of the boats, rafts or lifebelts was fitted with lights. As a result, many men were in the water for long after the point at which serious symptoms of hypothermia would have been expected.

Hertslet's lifeboat reached the *Darro* after about 50 minutes. Trapnell and the men hanging onto the upturned keel of No. 5 lifeboat were rescued after about an hour and a half. Yardley seems to have been in the water for about an hour and a half and so was probably becoming unconscious as a result of exposure. Matli may have been in the water for more than two and a half hours and, although he was able to talk to his rescuers, he was too cold to clamber up a rope ladder and fell back into the water. He told his rescuers that the man he had been clinging to on the raft, a Swazi, was 'dead cold' and semi-conscious – a clear sign of advanced hypothermia.

Matli described how some of the men who had died before the raft was found had been 'knocked out' by the water and had lain in the water 'with their backs up'.[36] This was probably because they had lost consciousness as a result of hypothermia and their lifebelts had failed to float them face up.

A failure in lifebelt drills?

The accounts of two auxiliary patrol boat captains that received a signal to go to the assistance of the *Mendi* may give us a further clue as to why so many died in this way. HMT *Grenadier* and HMT *Lucknow* were anchored in thick fog off Sandown Bay on the Isle of Wight when they received a wireless message to go to the assistance of the *Mendi*. At 8.15 am they hailed a schooner bound for Portsmouth whose crew said that they had heard cries to the south at 6.00 am. At 8.30 am, they sighted wreckage, including bunker hatches and spars. What they came across at 8.35 am is described as follows:

Sighted bodies of negroes dressed in military uniform, floating with aid of life-belts. A considerable number hanging on to tank rafts. Majority had their heads under water, their life-belts were made fast too low around their bodies, about the middle. Searched thoroughly, but on investigation there was not a live person among them. I estimate there were from 300 to 400 bodies. Among them were five white men, two of them apparently stewards, had their heads above water and well back, and arms outstretched as if they had been swimming on their backs. Hauled them aboard and found they were dead, no papers of identification on them. In searching found body of ship's 4th Officer. Papers found on body indicated that the officer's name was William Windsor Swall. Address on letter from Mother, The Haven, 4, Clarendon, Egremont, Cheshire, England. His head was under the water, chin on chest, one sea boot was off, hands tightly clenched.[37]

The captain of the *Grenadier* also saw three dead Labour Corps men lying on a life raft without lifebelts and completely naked. However, the real interest in his statement, also recorded in the ship's log, is that many of the men with their heads under water had secured their lifebelts around their waists. It therefore seems that many of the men drowned after losing consciousness in the advanced stages of hypothermia. Whether many more would have been saved had they worn their lifebelts correctly is unclear. Those men who lost consciousness were already in the very advanced stages of hypothermia. Some men, including Sergeant MacTavish, were hauled out of the water but still died, but it may be that many more could have survived.

Why so many men were not wearing their lifebelts correctly is unclear. Sergeant MacTavish and others talked about lifeboat drills being carried out during the voyage and it seems likely that the men of the Labour Corps would have been ordered to put their lifebelts on during these drills. Perhaps their officers did not know how to do that correctly and perhaps they were not supervised in doing this by the crew. It is clear from film shot on cross-channel troopships during the war that many men wore this type of lifebelt in this potentially dangerous way.[38]

In conclusion

While several factors contributed to cause the loss of life on the *Mendi*, it is still possible to understand why so many died. Although the evidence is not entirely clear, it does seem very likely that a significant number of men died as a direct result of the collision or drowned as holds 1 and 2 flooded. The *Mendi* was also very clearly not carrying enough lifeboats for the number of men on board. This and the crew's inability to launch all of them successfully meant that most of the men on deck had to take their chances by jumping into an abnormally cold sea. While most of them survived this because they were wearing lifebelts, the poor design of the life rafts of the time meant that the majority of the survivors had to remain in the water until they were rescued. The *Darro's* failure to join the rescue efforts, combined with the thick fog and darkness, meant that most of the men in the water died from hypothermia or drowning before they were found.

10

Dyobha: the man and a myth?

Isaac Dyobha's speech on the deck of the sinking ship and his exhortation to the doomed men to dance against death is the best-known aspect of the *Mendi* story. But who was this man and did the events reported really happen?

Who was Isaac Dyobha?

Isaac Williams Wauchope Dyobha was born on 17 July 1852 at Doornhoek near Uitenhage in what is now the Eastern Cape province of South Africa. He was the first-born son of William Wauchope Dyobha and Sabina Heka.[1] He entered the world at the height of the 8th Frontier War, or War of Mlangeni (1850–3), the penultimate convulsion in what has been described as 'Africa's 100 Years War', and shortly before the catastrophic Nonqawuse cattle killing of 1856–7.[2] Dyobha was born four months after the sinking of HMS *Birkenhead* off the Cape South Coast – the event that immortalised the maritime tradition of 'women and children first'. The *Birkenhead* was en route to the Eastern Cape when she was lost, carrying troop reinforcements and weapons for the Frontier War.[3]

The Frontier Wars were a series of nine separate conflicts in the Eastern Cape between 1779 and 1878, precipitated and fuelled by tensions created by European colonial expansion, and which dispossessed Xhosa and Khoikhoi people of their land and stock.[4] The cattle killing broke the dogged resistance to colonial expansion which the Xhosa had sustained for nearly 80 bitter years and effectively destroyed Xhosa power in the Eastern Cape, paving the way for their lands to be appropriated by the colonial government and handed out to white settlers. It is estimated that 400,000 cattle were slaughtered and, in the ensuing famine, between 20,000 and 40,000 Xhosa starved to death. Survivors abandoned their homes and land in search of food and many sought refuge across the Keiskamma River in the Cape Colony.[5]

This was the world of flux and change into which Dyobha was born. His father and grandfather had 'in the years preceding the radical changes [assailing] Xhosa society in the aftermath of the ... cattle killing, begun to acquaint themselves with the mores of "civilisation" as Christian converts'.[6]

His grandfather Citashe's life was indicative of the changes that placed a growing number of Xhosas at the intercept between tradition and the encroaching influences of European colonialism. Citashe was a follower of Nxele (otherwise known as Makhanda), the influential 'wardoctor' of Chief Ndlambe, who combined 'Christian millenarian thinking with the military aspirations of his people to forge a militant Xhosa nationalism'.[7] Citashe was converted to Christianity by Reverend John Ross of the Free Church at Ncerha (better known as Lovedale Mission) outside Alice in the Eastern Cape. Dyobha's father, Dyoba ka Citashe (Dyoba son of Citashe), received a formal, mission education at Lovedale, was christened William Wauchope on conversion and later in life was an elder at the Congregationalist Union Chapel.[8]

The young Dyobha was named Isaac, after his father's elder brother Yisake, and also Williams, after Joseph Williams, the missionary from the London Missionary Society who established the Kat River Mission in the Eastern Cape in 1816. Williams was the name Dyobha later used as his surname when he attended school at Lovedale Mission.[9]

Dyobha was schooled in Uitenhage and Port Elizabeth between 1857 and 1865. He then worked as a wool-washer before finding a job as a storeman in Port Elizabeth.[10] In 1874, he was sent to Lovedale College, where he proved to be a bright and talented student.[11] He earned his teacher's certificate in March 1875 and the following year volunteered to accompany Dr James Stewart, Principal of Lovedale College, on a missionary expedition to Nyasaland (modern Malawi) (Fig 10.1).[12] His participation in the trip was cut short by illness and he returned to the Eastern Cape in December 1877.

Dyobha had met his first wife, Naniwe, the daughter of John Lukalo, while he was at Lovedale, where she was an assistant in the boys' boarding house. They were married in Uitenhage, in April 1878, and the marriage produced three daughters – Grisell, Jubilee and Jessie – and a son, Isaac (Fig 10.2).[13]

The 1880s were a significant decade in the development of a nascent black political culture in the Eastern Cape. Dyobha and his contemporaries, 'the small missionary educated class of Africans which had emerged by the 1870s', were convinced of the futility of continuing to oppose white colonial expansion through war, and sought new means of protesting African interests.[14]

Dyobha's background and education – as the third generation of a family of Christian converts – gave him a 'strong stamp of colonial culture, religion and mores'. It also gave him the confidence 'to challenge some of the iniquities of colonial rule, using its own instruments – literacy, schooling, the legal system [and] political organisations'.[15] Dyobha believed that Xhosa-speakers could win an equal place for themselves in Cape

Fig 10.1 Dyobha (front right) and colleagues in Malawian mission venture.
[African Media Online/Cory Library 275_24]

colonial society and that the justness of this cause would see it triumph, despite the growing tide of racial discrimination in the Cape from the 1880s.[16]

He grew to be a figure of public prominence as a writer, thinker and activist within South Africa's black community, particularly in the Eastern Cape,[17] and became involved in electoral politics. Early in 1881, it was rumoured that he planned to stand for the Cape Parliament, which still had a limited black franchise, at the next election, but this never happened.[18] After teaching in Uitenhage for some years following his return from Malawi, he took a job in Port Elizabeth in 1882 as a clerk and interpreter at the Resident Magistrate's Court.[19] In Port Elizabeth, he threw himself

Fig 10.2 Dyobha and family. [African Media Online/Cory Library 150_56]

into political and social activism. He was a Sunday school teacher, a strong
supporter of the temperance movement, a lay preacher and a prolific
contributor to the burgeoning black press. In September 1882, he was
a founding member and the first chairperson of Imbumba Yamanyama
(South African Aborigines Association), one of the earliest black cultural
and political organisations in South Africa.[20]

Imbumba was formed in response to the establishment, in 1881, of the
Afrikaner Bond, an anti-imperialist, republican union of two nationalist
Afrikaner organisations, the *Genootskap vir Regte Afrikaners* (Society of
True Afrikaners) and *Zuidafrikaansche Boeren Beschermings Vereeniging*
(South African Farmers' Protection Association),[21] which was perceived

as a threat to black African interests. Dyobha and the other founders of Imbumba identified the same need to create pan-ethnic nationalism among black South Africans as white Afrikaners envisaged under the Afrikaner Bond.[22] Dyobha's address to the opening meeting of Imbumba is interesting in that it is reminiscent of the words attributed to him as the *Mendi* sank. He stressed the need for unity among black South Africans, saying 'let this mbumba[23] gather different factions – let it assemble the Xhosa and the Mfengu and the Zulu and the Sotho'.[24]

In 1888, Dyobha was called to the ministry and returned to Lovedale College to study theology. He was ordained as a Pastor in the Congregational Native Church in March 1892 and was sent to minister to the congregations of Fort Beaufort and Blinkwater, which he served for 15 years.[25]

In 1908, Dyobha was charged with falsifying the will of one of his parishioners, Sarah Tshona. For a period before Tshona's death in 1905, Dyobha had taken on the responsibility of managing her estate and a will was said to have been made of which he was the designated executor. The will left the bulk of her land and property to her second son, which led to suspicions regarding its authenticity. The family challenged it in court, and Dyobha was drawn into a lengthy civil case that ended with him being given a three-year jail sentence for fraud and forgery. He served two years in prison in Cape Town between 1910 and 1912.[26] His wife Naniwe died in 1911, while he was in prison.

After his release, he returned to the Eastern Cape, where he continued his ministry and resumed his political activities. For reasons related to political allegiances, he absented himself from some of the seminal political events in the Eastern Cape in the years after his release from prison. This included, on 8 January 1912, the formative meeting of the South African Native National Congress, the organisation that took the van of black South African politics up to, during and following the First World War, and was renamed the African National Congress in 1923.[27]

Dyobha's lifelong belief in education for black South Africans resulted in his serving on the committee of the Inter-State Native College scheme, which in 1916 oversaw the establishment of the South African Native College on a site adjacent to Lovedale. The college became the University of Fort Hare and counts among its alumni Nelson Mandela, Oliver Tambo, Robert Sobukwe, Desmond Tutu, Kenneth Kaunda, Seretse Khama, Robert Mugabe, Joshua Nkomo and Julius Nyerere.[28]

Dyobha married Gqunukhwebe, the daughter of Saul Koom, in 1913 and seems to have lived at Knapps Hope, east of Alice until late in 1916, when he enlisted in the SANLC as an interpreter and was sent to the transit camp at Rosebank in Cape Town.[29] He was then 64 years of age (Fig 10.3).

Fig 10.3 Dyobha as an elderly man. [South African National Museum of Military History]

According to Mqhayi's obituary for Dyobha, he was well regarded by the white officers of the SANLC in Rosebank and remained at the camp for a couple of months to help orientate and train recruits as they arrived.[30] Then, in late January 1917, Dyobha and more than 800 other members of the SANLC made their way from Rosebank, around the shoulder of Devil's Peak and down to Cape Town Docks to board the *Mendi* for France. Four weeks later, Dyobha died when the *Mendi* sank, apparently in circumstances that have since come to define the event and have immortalised both him and the *Mendi*.

Dyobha's speech and the 'death dance'

In January 1936, in an obituary to Dyobha, the celebrated Xhosa poet, praise singer and historian Samuel E K Mqhayi identified Dyobha as the hero who had rallied the men on the decks of the sinking *Mendi* before leading them in a death dance:

> Those who were there say the hero from Ngqika's land, descended from heroes, was standing to one side now as the ship was sinking! As a chaplain he had the opportunity to board a boat and save himself, but he didn't! He was appealing to the leaderless soldiers urging them to stay calm, to die like heroes on their way to war. We hear that he said:
> Now then stay calm my countrymen! Calmly face your death!

This is what you came to do! This is why you left your homes!
Peace, our own brave warriors! Peace, you sons of heroes, today is your
final day, prepare for the ultimate ford!

As he spoke he burst into his people's anthem![31]

This was not the first time that there had been public reference made
to both a rallying speech and a death dance on the deck of the *Mendi* as
it sank. It was, however, the most detailed reporting of these events and
the most explicit linking of Dyobha with them. What is interesting about
Mqhayi's references to events related to Dyobha, however, is that they
suggest he wasn't reporting something new; rather, his choice of words
suggests that these events were commonly known, the telling thereof
brought back to South Africa by 'those who were there'. Two years earlier,
in March 1934, an article in *Umteteli wa bantu* (*Mouthpiece of the People*),
a moderate black newspaper established by the South African Chamber of
Mines and the Native Recruiting Corporation after the 1920 mineworkers
strike, identified Dyobha as a hero of the *Mendi* who encouraged the
doomed troops.[32] Prior to these newspaper stories, there had been
statements at public events associated with the commemoration of the
Mendi that singled Dyobha out as having played a special role in the events
surrounding the sinking of the ship.

From 1931, annual commemorations of the disaster were organised
at various places in South Africa. Contemporary figures such as A B
Xuma, R V Selope Thema and Jan Hofmeyer addressed these meetings,
and survivors offered reminiscences. At a *Mendi* memorial service in
Johannesburg in 1932, Dr Lewis E Herslet, the SANLC medical officer
aboard the *Mendi*, praised Dyobha's 'valuable work' in a speech he gave.[33]
While Herslet's words could simply have been general praise for the role
Dyobha had played in the corps, they may also hint at his involvement
in something larger and as yet not fully in the public eye. As a survivor of
the sinking of the *Mendi*, Herslet may have been privy to other survivors'
individual experiences of the event, so may have been aware of any
accounts of events involving Dyobha on the morning the *Mendi* sank.

This begs the question: if Dyobha did, in fact, inspire his comrades
with a speech and then lead a dance on the deck as the *Mendi* sank, why
should this have taken so long to be publicly reported? One explanation
may be that the delay was simply because the story, carried home by
Mendi survivors and then retold and passed among the families and
communities of those aboard the ship, becoming part of the oral history of
the *Mendi* and the SANLC, took this long to reach the ears of journalists.
In the debate over the truth of the story, some have chosen to go with
tradition, 'believing that there may be a solid core of truth in the story'.[34]

Others are of the view that 'in the absence of persuasive evidence it would be misleading to accept the tale at face value'.[35] This view suggests that the story was, in the most part, a fiction, a tale created around an iconic, potentially unifying event for black South Africans, to exploit for political reasons the power of the loss of the *Mendi* and what it meant. Perhaps, however, the truth lies somewhere in between: a small kernel of fact, embroidered and embellished into the story that has become mythic.

What is known is that Dyobha was substantially older than the majority of SANLC recruits. As an elder in black South African society and as a clergyman, he would thus have represented an immediate and obvious authority figure to the panicked and frightened men crowding onto the deck of the *Mendi* after the collision with the *Darro*. He was someone to whom the other men are likely to have looked for guidance and reassurance, as the unfamiliar path they were embarked upon suddenly turned deadly dangerous. It is possible, perhaps even likely, that he responded by offering words of comfort and reassurance to calm and soothe men who, like himself, probably knew they were about to die.

If he did make some sort of speech, it is probably unlikely that it took the form of the rousing, ringing cry across the deck most often described in the telling of the *Mendi* story. Although some accounts of the sinking suggest that the men were very disciplined in their reaction to the collision, others, such as Marks Mokoena, describe a more chaotic scene: one of 'great panic and confusion [with] … men plunged into the rough, cold water, singing, praying and crying'.[36] This was not a situation in which stirring speeches are likely to have been made to a large audience.

Instead, it is more likely that Dyobha's audience was a small group of men within the wider, milling mass on the deck of the *Mendi*: men who, perhaps, hung back after the order to abandon ship had been given, unwilling to leave the relative safety of the deck for the unknown, fog-shrouded water beyond.

If Dyobha did speak, what did he say to those around him? Did he use the rhetoric of black nationalism, as the stories tell, or did he say a prayer? Given all that is known about the sinking of the *Mendi*, this was not an event that inspired heroic grandstanding. It was instead a few minutes during which a large number of men, who were a very long way from home in very alien circumstances, had to face their own mortality. As a clergyman, it is very likely that whatever Dyobha said reflected this fact, and provided simple words to reassure and calm.

The speed with which the *Mendi* sank after the collision is also a consideration in the reports that the men then danced on the deck. Little more than 20 minutes elapsed from the time of impact to the *Mendi* disappearing below the water. As the sea rushed into the ruptured hull of the ship and the bow sank, so the deck, which was slick and slippery from the fog, sloped ever more steeply and the ship took on a heavy list to starboard. Men who chose not to leave the ship and remained on the deck probably had to hang onto anything they could find to stay upright and prevent themselves from being pitched into the sea. Seen in this light, it seems unlikely that they would have been able to dance, a conclusion supported by the fact that a dance was not reported in any of the testimonies of survivors of the sinking.

The *Birkenhead* and the *Mendi*

Why, then, did these stories come to be associated with the *Mendi*? The story of the speech and dance are about men choosing to stay on the *Mendi* and die together. This has an interesting echo in an event already referred to in this chapter – the sinking of the *Birkenhead* just over 60 years earlier.

Like the *Mendi*, the *Birkenhead* was carrying troops and, again like the *Mendi*, it sank very quickly. When it became clear that the *Birkenhead* was lost, the women and children aboard were put into the available boats. To avoid a rush on the boats, the officer commanding the troops ordered them to form up on the deck and they stood together in their ranks as the ship sank, taking most of them with it. These actions resulted in the loss of this ordinary troopship becoming an iconic event and created one of the abiding traditions of the modern world – that of 'women and children first' in the event of a disaster.

There are similarities in the reported actions of those on the decks of the *Birkenhead* and the *Mendi*, events that occurred within living memory of each other. Could the *Mendi* speech and death dance have been modelled on the *Birkenhead* – either by Dyobha, who, with his western schooling, is likely to have known the *Birkenhead* story and seen the similarity as he faced death with his fellow troops on the deck of the *Mendi* that cold morning, or by those who added to the story of the event in the years following the sinking of the *Mendi*? Certainly, this conflation of the two events seems to have crept into some recent descriptions of the loss of the *Mendi*. Grundlingh quotes the South African Minister of Arts and Culture, Pallo Jordan, at the time of the *Mendi* 90th anniversary commemorations in 2007 describing how the men 'bravely stood to attention, performed a dance and went down with their ship'.[37]

The power of the myth

It will probably never be possible to prove definitively whether Dyobha actually made a speech on the deck that morning or whether the SANLC men danced. These two scenes have, however, become a vital and undeniable part of the story of the *Mendi*. They have also played a role in the politics of 20th-century South Africa and have increasingly been claimed in the post-apartheid era as a reminder of the sacrifices that black South Africans made in a colonial and post-colonial milieu in the fight for political freedom and social justice. That they still have a resonance in South Africa today is clear from the high political profile the *Mendi* enjoys, demonstrated by the naming of two naval vessels to commemorate the event, the renaming of the national civilian order for bravery as the Order of *Mendi*,[38] and the choice of 21 February – the date the ship went down – as South Africa's annual Armed Forces Day.

Grundlingh points out that, in the end, even if the story of the speech and death dance is a myth, that in itself is part of what makes the *Mendi* so important – in the past and in the present. He quotes Ralph Samuel and Paul Thompson: 'Myths open up a history which refuses to be safely boxed away in card indexes or computer programs: which instead pivots on the *active* relationship between past and present, subjective and objective, poetic and political.'[39] Grundlingh sees the *Mendi*, as the story is told today, as embodying the need to construct a myth around wartime service and disaster 'to lay claims to bravery and ... to invest the event with the weight of historicity which could serve a useful purpose in the present'.[40] Could it not be that the stories that developed around the loss of the *Mendi* give the men who died that foggy morning an active voice and an agency that the context of a time – the SANLC and the political situation in South Africa – tried to deny them? The events reported on the deck of the *Mendi* can also be seen as a metaphor for the wider SANLC experience, where men required by the system to accept a passive role became active participants and agents in the system by subverting the controls and strictures that tried to enforce their passivity. It is perhaps as a reflection of the resistance by members of the SANLC to passively accepting their fate that the greatest power of the *Mendi* resides.

As for Isaac Dyobha – whether the clergyman, intellectual and activist who enlisted in the SANLC as a concrete demonstration of his beliefs, or the orator on the deck around whom the myth of the *Mendi* has developed – he was, like many other members of South Africa's early 20th-century educated black elite, a man who straddled two worlds. His life and activities were characterised and defined by his efforts to come to terms with his and his people's intellectual, social and political hybridity and divided loyalties in a changing colonial world. He was a complex man who reflected in his life and death the dual loyalties of black South African society.[41]

11
Foreign labour on the Western Front: the common experience

By January 1917, the initial quota of 10,000 labourers promised by the South African Government had been recruited and dispatched by sea to France. During the next 18 months, another 11,000 black South Africans would follow.

The SANLC was but a small cog in the huge international machine dedicated to meeting the British Army's labour needs during the First World War. At the same time as the SANLC, other foreign labour corps were pouring into France from across the world until, together, these corps numbered 195,000 men in November 1918.

South Africa's insistence on the special standards and restrictions required for its labourers would suggest that the SANLC cog was slightly different from all the other cogs that kept the war machinery working. But was this the case, and was the experience of the SANLC the same as or different from that of the other foreign labour also deployed in France, especially the Chinese and Egyptians? As this chapter will show, despite their diverse origins, the experiences of the foreign labour corps on the Western Front were remarkably similar, and in many respects were marked by both overt and covert discrimination.

European attitudes to foreign labour

In the planning for and creation of the SANLC, the War Office had been required to tailor its needs to the demands of British organised labour, who were opposed to the deployment of foreign labour within the UK because of possible impacts on British jobs. The same applied to Chinese labour.[1] The result was that, with the exception of a small number of skilled Chinese labourers, all other foreign war labour was employed outside the UK.

Although the exclusion of foreign labour can be viewed as a simple economic concern around job security for British workers, foreign labourers appear to have experienced a regime of difference and discrimination during their wartime service that had nothing to do with economics. The wartime experience of foreign labour corps on the Western Front was deeply bound up in contemporary British attitudes to race and class. There was a perception that these foreign labourers were in some way inferior to Britons that runs like a common thread through the experience of the South Africans, the Chinese and the Egyptians on the Western Front. These attitudes manifested themselves in the everyday minutiae of the foreign labour corps experience: in the second-rate, non-military uniforms the various corps were issued, in their food rations and in the closed camps or compounds in which they were housed. They also made themselves apparent in the racist attitudes of those commanding the corps. The treatment of the foreign labour corps left much to be desired and their service went largely unacknowledged. Ultimately, wearing the uniform did not win them respect as 'real' soldiers.[2] The result was a state of simmering discontent within the labour corps, which flashed into unrest and mutiny with increasing regularity as the war proceeded.

Reasons for enlisting

Before exploring the common wartime experiences of these foreign labourers, it is worth touching on areas of commonality in their establishment and recruitment.

Just like black South Africans, Egyptian *fellahin*[3] were a politically and economically marginalised group in a country under a colonial administration. It can be expected that similar political and economic drivers to those already discussed for South Africa (*see* Chapter 3) would have been central to the recruitment and enlistment of Egyptian labourers into the ELC (Fig 11.1). By contrast, for Chinese labourers recruitment was much more an economic transaction, because China was a sovereign power and, at that stage, not involved in the war. That said, it is clear from the earlier discussion of the politics of the CLC (*see* Chapter 2) that the Chinese Government had specific geopolitical reasons for supporting the scheme, albeit covertly.

British subjects from other parts of the world viewed their participation in a similar way to the black South Africans who supported the formation of the SANLC in the hope that this would translate into political change after the war. For example, West Indian middle-class blacks – who were supporting the creation of a fighting regiment rather than a labour corps – 'were aware of the relevance of the war in their struggle for political and constitutional change ... [and there] was a clear linkage between their support for the war effort and the grant of the reforms they desired'.[4]

Fig 11.1 Egyptian Labour Corps handling stores at the quay, Boulogne, 12 August 1917. [© Imperial War Museum Q2703]

Common terms of employment

The conditions of employment of the various foreign labour corps were similar. Recruits were hired on fixed-term contracts: a year in the case of the South Africans, six or seven months for the Egyptians and three or five years in the case of the Chinese.[5] Conditions were onerous, with the labourers expected to work 10 hours a day and, in the case of the Chinese contingent, seven days a week.[6] They received a daily wage, the greatest part of which was automatically remitted to their families every month, or deferred, to be paid out on completion of their contracts. The scale of pay for the SANLC was somewhat higher than the going rate for labourers in South Africa and many *fellahin* may also have sought employment in the ELC because it paid relatively well.[7]

Members of all three of these foreign labour corps were provided with clothing and a daily food ration, and were accommodated in specially constructed camps. However, the uniforms they were issued, problems associated with their rations and the closed compounds in which they were housed proved to be a source of immediate and ongoing dissatisfaction, unhappiness and unrest within the SANLC, and similar issues marked the employment of both the Chinese and Egyptians in France.[8] A major source of friction for many Chinese labourers was the brass identity disc each received. These were permanently attached on a chain around the recruit's wrist by a blacksmith and were regarded as an affront and a gross humiliation by the more sophisticated and educated members of the corps.[9]

Contradictory interpretations of the terms of the employment contracts by South African and Egyptian labourers, on the one hand, and the military authorities managing them, on the other, also proved to be a serious source of friction, and in more than one instance resulted in bloodshed.[10] The common denominator that perhaps had the most marked impact on the wartime experience of all the foreign labour contingents was that these units were subject to military law. The members of the foreign labour corps were recruited and enlisted as labourers, not soldiers, yet they were managed in terms of, and were subject to, military discipline under the Army Act, including field punishments and courts martial, conviction at which could carry the death penalty.[11] The use of beating and the lash was common as a means of disciplining men. Although it was a brutal time, and the Western Front a brutal place, the manner in which the military authorities dealt with what were legitimate labour disputes with the foreign labourers was, nevertheless, heavy-handed and insensitive.

Areas of deployment

Another common feature of the foreign labour corps was the stipulation in their terms of employment that they were to be employed outside the combat zone, in areas away from the front lines. An exception was the Indian labour units, which were involved in building fortifications and transporting munitions closer to the front, and the British labour companies and units, which also performed their duties in forward areas, often coming under enemy fire.[12]

As was made clear in Chapter 6, deployment of the foreign labour corps in the Lines of Communication, away from the front, was not always possible or desirable, and even when these units were deployed in the rear, they were not immune from attack. In addition to the war-diary evidence already quoted, a range of writers cite instances of South African, Chinese and Egyptian labour units suffering shelling or bombing during air raids.[13] Such exposure to hostile fire should not be surprising and was perhaps inevitable when units were deployed near the front or at the Channel ports, which were the targets of German artillery and aircraft attacks.

The labour corps may, however, have been targeted for attack because of the vital role in the war effort they were perceived by the Germans as playing. A particularly sinister expression of this is suggested by the experiences of a South African unit stationed near Dieppe in 1917. An SANLC veteran recounted an attack on his unit's camp by German aircraft that dropped bombs and propaganda leaflets addressed to the black labourers. The pamphlets read: 'In this war I hate black people the most. I do not know what they want in this European war. Where I find them, I will smash them'.[14] The use of pre-prepared leaflets suggests this was part of a wider propaganda campaign.

Segregation and the closed-compound system

On an operational level, the deployment of the foreign labour corps behind the lines, rather than at the front, can be understood in terms of the *raison d'être* of these corps and the nature of their service location. However, there were other reasons for employing foreign labourers behind the front and these were, to a large degree, based on the requirement to keep them segregated from other units.

The closed-compound system was one with which the South African Government in 1917 was very familiar, and it is hardly surprising that it travelled to France with the South African labour contingent. Grundlingh suggests that 'of all the labour contingents in France ... the SANLC was the only one to be housed in compounds [and that] only the German prisoners-of-war ... were likewise confined'.[15] However, the system seems to have been readily embraced by the British authorities and applied to the other foreign labour corps. The Chinese and Egyptian Labour Corps, and in all likelihood some or all of the other foreign labour corps, were also intentionally segregated and housed in camps very similar to those of the black South Africans.[16]

The decision to apply the closed-compound system to the Chinese Labour Corps seems to have been the result of a War Office conference in February 1917 to consider how Chinese labour would be handled. In addition to discussing the work to which Chinese labourers would be put, the meeting decided that the men of the corps would need to be kept isolated from the rest of the army 'because the coolies' unusual and exotic origins and unknown temperaments might make them the butt of considerable racial discrimination'.[17] Thus, a later description of one of the Chinese labour hospitals refers to a 'barbed wire fence, eight feet high, which surrounded each perimeter. These fences were patrolled and guarded' (Fig 11.2).[18]

The layout and construction of the foreign labour compounds differed in only minor details from the layout and construction of British military prisons on the Western Front: camps such as No. 1 Military Prison, Blargies North, near Abancourt.[19] The success of the design of a British

M. M. 6 MONT KEMMEL   de la Guerre 1914-18. Camp Chinois (Annamites britanniques)
Br,   Souvenir Van den Oorlog   Kamp van Chinoezen (Engelsche annamiten)
                                                Of the War   Chinese (Pekin) Camp British

Fig 11.2 CLC camp with Nissen huts, 'Pekin Camp' in Belgium. [© Mary Evans]

army prison camp built near Rouen to accommodate 600 military prisoners led to the layout of this camp being chosen by the Director of Military Prisons as the type plan for future prison camps on the Western Front.

The similarity between the form of the British military prisons and the foreign labour corps compounds is not surprising. The British military authorities had been in discussions with the South African Government since mid-1916 about the requirements for the accommodation for the SANLC, and had been provided with detailed specifications for the camps required. In fact, by late 1916, the Directorate of Labour had produced an Appendix to Notes for Officer of Labour Companies (South African Native Labour).[20] They must have been aware of what a well-refined system of control the closed-compound system of the South African mines represented and, based on this, it is not unreasonable to view the correspondence between the design of the labour corps compounds and British military prison camps as no accident.

The labour camps were blatantly discriminatory and degraded those who were forced to occupy them through the total control of movement they imposed. They left a deep impression on the members of the SANLC. In the words of one veteran, 'the compounds ... cannot be forgotten as they were like prisons'.[21] Yet philanthropic bodies, such as the Aborigines Protection Society of London, accepted and approved of the compound system as a necessary measure for the 'welfare' of Africans in a foreign environment. Without questioning the assumptions underlying the compound system, members of the Society who visited the camps reported 'in the best traditions of paternalism that they were impressed by the way in which Africans were cared for'.[22] The official descriptions of the camps are also painted in glowing terms and give the impression of a happy and contented labour force. But within a very short space of time after arriving in France, the SANLC, CLC and ELC all experienced labour unrest and strikes.

Labour unrest

That there would be labour unrest within the various foreign labour corps should not have been surprising, given the conditions under which they served and the range of men recruited into the various corps. In addition to the unskilled labourers who made up the bulk of those recruited, the corps also included literate, articulate and well-educated men 'capable of organising and representing others with little or no previous experience of collective bargaining'.[23]

The main thrust of SANLC resistance to the conditions in France, which began as early as March 1917 when members of an SANLC company in Dieppe went on strike, was directed at the closed-compound system, although there was also dissatisfaction with clothing, food and other contract terms (Fig 11.3). An SANLC officer wrote: 'a great cry that is heard from many of the Companies is against the compounding'. He goes on to say that 'my natives have said nothing of this to me so that I think that many of the Basuthos [sic] are taking their cue from educated natives of other Provinces who certainly have made the compound system their chief grievance', which bears out the role probably played by the more educated members of the corps in formulating grievances and directing resistance.[24]

These same issues were the drivers of, and the focus of resistance and defiance by, the other labour corps such as the Egyptians who were engaged in collective protests in northern France from late May 1917.[25]

During 1917 and 1918 there was ongoing and persistent labour unrest in many foreign labour corps camps, which in a number of cases resulted in the death of some of those involved. This was usually as a result of the way the military dealt with what were, for the most part, genuine grievances by the labourers.

A litany of labour disputes and strikes by the various labour corps presents a starkly contrasting picture to the official word of conditions within the foreign labour corps. For example, Egyptian workers at a camp in Marseilles were involved in a spontaneous revolt over repatriation at the expiry of their contracts. The uprising was brutally suppressed and one of the labourers involved was court martialled and executed.[26]

Fig 11.3 SANLC members in a camp in France. [© National Library of Scotland]

By early 1918, morale in many of the Chinese units was also very low. Labourers were penned in their segregated and guarded compounds and there had been a number of incidents of unrest. On 16 December 1917, there was a 'serious disturbance' at a Chinese Labour Corps camp at Fontinettes. A protest by the labourers over bullying by British NCOs was broken up when their armed guard fired on them, killing four and wounding nine. On Christmas Day 1917, Chinese labourers turned on and killed an NCO who had been an extortioner and also too liberal with the lash. They then broke out of their camp but were pursued by local British army units. Eight were shot, three fatally, and 93 were imprisoned after being captured.[27]

The results of unrest in SANLC camps are recorded in medical reports from corps hospitals, one of which refers to 'death by accidental shooting'.[28] Far from being accidental, the incident in question took place near Dieppe on 23 July 1917 at No. 7 camp, sparked off by the arrest of a labourer who refused to obey an order to wash his clothes only within the compound:

[He] was brought before the Officer Commanding the Camp on a charge of refusing to obey the order of a British NCO, ... awarded 7 days Field Punishment No. 1 and placed in the Guard Tent. Subsequently the men of the platoon to which the man belonged forced the guard and released the man. This overt action of insubordination coupled with signs of general unrest among the men of the prisoner's Company led the Officer Commanding to call for an armed guard to be sent to the Camp. On the arrival of this Guard the prisoner was rearrested and marched out of the Camp. The men of the prisoner's platoon showing signs of creating further trouble were also arrested and marched out of the Camp. A general rush was then made upon the gate by the men of the other Companies in the Camp. The gate was held by Officers and NCOs of SANLC but they were overpowered and the gate was forced. The Armed Guard, now outside the Camp, fired upon the gate to prevent the mass of natives coming out of the Camp, with the result that casualties occurred both to the Natives and British personnel.[29]

Four members of the SANLC died from gunshot wounds and 11 were injured. The Commonwealth War Graves cemetery at Arques la Bataille near Dieppe contains the graves of four members of the SANLC who died on 23 July 1917 – Privates Robbie Matsamai (Service No. 10003), Frans Nteke (No. 12512), Jonas Motseke (No. 12448) and Piet Malisela (No. 12533) – and it seems likely that these are the men killed during the Dieppe incident.[30] The incident was not reported in South Africa.[31]

Earlier that year, on 27 February 1917, SANLC labourers at No. 10 Camp, Valancine, 'joined in a disturbance of a mutinous nature, in the course of which there was violence to their superiors and prisoners released from confinement', while unhappiness about the expiry of contracts led to strikes among SANLC companies at Abancourt and Rouen in October 1917.[32]

The common theme in the handling of these incidents is the summary and heavy-handed nature of the military response to labour disputes and grievances over conditions expressed by members of a contracted labour force: they were dealt with in terms of military law and those involved were accused of mutiny. This was perhaps to be expected, given the context of the war. However, it does seem from reports and descriptions of the incidents that there was more than a hint of racism and intolerance involved in the way they were handled, which is perhaps indicative of the prevailing attitudes to non-Europeans.

SANLC resistance to control

Persistent and effective resistance to the compound system within the SANLC increased, and incidents of 'unruly behaviour' became so frequent that, as 1917 dragged into 1918, it became increasingly difficult for the authorities to maintain the compound system.

The archival evidence associated with the SANLC, much of it written by the officers and other white officials with a vested interest in the success of the scheme, suggests that if the men 'did not actually welcome the disciplinary measures and various restrictions, they certainly accepted these passively'. Grundlingh suggests that while outwardly most acquiesced, this does not imply compliance.[33]

Lieutenant-Colonel Godley, second-in-command of the SANLC, admitted in a confidential letter in late 1917 that 'the temper of a large proportion of the men is distinctly nasty' and that there was a 'constant undercurrent of feeling among the Natives that they of all the King's soldiers are singled out for differential treatment'.[34] He conceded in the same letter that 'it is unfair to ask, or even allow men to bind themselves down indefinitely under conditions which are unique, as all other units in France, both white and black, are free to move about'. He pointed out the 'impossibility of expecting any human beings to work … in such surroundings without occasional relaxation and change, which under the close compound system it is next to impossible to secure them'.[35] In his opinion, serious consideration should be given to abandoning the closed-compound system. But because the compounds were the cornerstone of the SANLC as a workable and acceptable concept to South Africans, their abandonment in favour of a less restrictive system was not possible.

As a result, despite the best efforts of the South African authorities to enforce absolute control over the men of the SANLC, many members of the corps found ways of flouting or subverting these strictures. In some cases, labourers used resistance as leverage to try and manipulate their conditions. For example, Private Albert Mboniswa was punished for 'failing to carry out his duties and stating he was unable to [do so] unless supplied with beer, as furnished to European troops', and one SANLC company refused their allocated food and demanded that they receive the same rations as white troops.[36]

Examples of 'punishments affecting pay' in Table 11.1, taken from Daily Orders of just one SANLC unit, offer further insights into the ways in which the men of the corps pushed back against the controls placed on them.[37]

From the number of cases of men escaping camp bounds, it can be suggested that hospital camps, at least, were considerably more porous and much less secure than the South African authorities desired.

Dry canteens and recreation rooms in each compound, and the cold climate, were also believed by one SANLC officer to provide 'a certain guarantee against immorality' within the corps.[38] The reality was quite different.

Although 'kaffir beer',[39] which was recommended by one SANLC Medical Officer for 'regular issue to all compounds for its anti-scorbutic

Table 11.1 Daily Orders SANLC Medical Section No. 3 – Punishment Affecting Pay

28/02/1917	5399 Sgt Alfred Mikani	Tried by F. General Court Martial … for 'being found beyond the limits fixed by orders without a pass or written leave from his Commanding Officer'	Reduced to the ranks and 21 days F.P. No. 2
03/06/1917	Pte William	Breaking camp 20h45	Forfeits 10/-
09/06/1917	4491 3rd Class Orderly Albert	Breaking camp 20h00	Forfeits 10/-
10/07/1917	582 Pte Andries 11241 Pte Johannes	Breaking out of barracks between 21h30 [on] 09/07/1917 and 05h30 [on] 10/07/1917	14 days F.P. No. 1
06/08/1917	Pte Conan	Being found in possession of spirits	Awarded 10 days F.P. No. 1
13/08/1917	556 1st Class Orderly, Amos	Being absent from his ward Being in possession of intoxicating liquor	Forfeits 1 pound and reduced grading of 3rd Class Orderly
13/08/1917	11160 Pte Johnson	Absent from duty Rendering himself unfit for duty by drinking intoxicating liquor	Forfeits 2 pounds
19/10/1017	1st Class Orderly Alvern F.S.	Absent from No. 1 Rest Camp Out of bounds	Forfeits 5 days' pay
22/10/1917	1st Class Orderly Albert	In town without a pass	Forfeits 1 day's pay
11/10/1918	Pte Johnson	Breaking out of camp at 10pm and remaining absent until midnight	Forfeits 40/-

properties', was brewed for the corps, other liquor was strictly forbidden to SANLC labourers.[40] As the Daily Orders listed in Table 11.1 show, however, the men still managed to obtain alcohol and over-indulge, the SANLC Rouen Health Report for December 1917 listing 'twelve cases of alcoholism … at No. 1 Camp … and one death'. Officers were also requested to keep an eye out for 'dagga' (marijuana), which was often smuggled from South Africa by the labourers.[41]

A case of venereal disease, contracted in France, is noted in the same health report. The medical officer notes that 'the patient had been working in night duty at the docks in Rouen and late in the evening he had exposed himself to the infection'. One can guess how that exposure occurred and it suggests that the measures to isolate the corps from local inhabitants, particularly women, were not watertight. A letter from the South African Chief Censor to the Acting Secretary for Defence notifying him that he had 'condemned a number of letters from French women to natives', and another to the Chief Postal Censor in London asking him to 'be so good as to cause the correspondence between English or Scotch women and the members of the Native Labour Corps to be stopped', also suggest an undesired permeability in the carefully constructed, tightly bound ideal of control of the SANLC.[42]

12

The end of the experiment and after

As new outbreaks of unrest and disputes over the repatriation of labourers from France at the expiry of their contracts escalated in early 1918, and negative pressure generated by the labour corps 'experiment' grew at home, the South African Government appears to have lost its resolve and disengaged the SANLC, shipping the contingent home to be disbanded.

The official reason given was that the SANLC was no longer practicable due to 'shipping shortages and the exigencies of war'.[1] Ultimately, however, the scheme's failure – not a word used by the South African authorities – came down to the men of the SANLC. Their acts of resistance, both small and large, undermined the controls insisted upon by the Government. Once the compound system, initially held up as the picture of success, was no longer risk-free, the only choice for a government unwilling to compromise was to terminate the scheme.

Official notice of the end of recruitment in South Africa was sent to all magistrates, native commissioners and officials of the Department of Native Affairs on 3 December 1917 by Lieutenant-Colonel Godley, in a circular which read:

> In view of the shortage of shipping and consequent difficulty of repatriation within the period of contract, the Army Council has intimated that it finds itself unable to accept any further Natives for the South African Native Labour corps beyond those already recruited. You are therefore requested to take immediate steps to stop all recruiting for the SANLC. All persons, both European and native, engaged in recruiting, should be immediately withdrawn from this duty and their services dispensed with, and in this connection all Native members of the corps should be returned to the Depot for discharge.[2]

When recruiting formally ended in January 1918, there were a few thousand men at the Rosebank depot waiting to travel to France.[3] These men had to be told their services were no longer required and that they could return home.

The type of unrest within the SANLC described in the previous chapter continued even as men were shipped home from France. On 15 November 1917, for example, Basuto members of the SANLC aboard the transport

Miltiades refused to obey an order given by Zulu military policemen within the corps, on the grounds that their contract had expired and they were thus no longer subject to SANLC discipline. One man was killed and another wounded during the fracas that ensued, and eight men were court martialled and convicted when the *Miltiades* reached Cape Town: one was sentenced to 12 years imprisonment, the remainder 10 years, all with hard labour. Prime Minister Botha and Governor-General Buxton considered the sentences excessive and persuaded Brigadier-General Martyn, the British Officer Commanding South Africa Military Command, to order the release of the prisoners in May 1918.[4]

The last ship with 280 SANLC repatriates left France for Cape Town on the 6 September 1918.[5]

In total, 20,887 black men and NCOs, 238 white officers and 960 white NCOs served with the SANLC in France. The (former) Transvaal province provided the largest number of SANLC members – about 13,500. Roughly 7,000 recruits came from the (former) Cape Province, mainly from the Eastern Cape, 1,500 from Natal and the remainder from the Orange Free State and the various British protectorates in southern Africa.[6]

Table 12.1 Statistical Return respecting natives of the SANLC[7]

Number of men embarked from South Africa:	20,887
Repatriated to South Africa as time expired:	18,883
Repatriated to South Africa as medically unfit:	1,025
Repatriated from hospital in Sierra Leone	6
Lost on HMT *Mendi*:	607
Died at sea en route to Europe:	14
Died in Europe – various causes:	307
Died in Europe – result of accidents:	10
Transferred to Portuguese Army:	1
Transferred to Cape Auxiliary Horse Transport:	15
Awaiting disposal:	19
Total accounted for:	20,887

Black post-war expectations and realities in South Africa

Following the disbanding of the SANLC, its members were returned to South Africa, where they and other black South Africans were to be bitterly disappointed in their expectations of what their wartime service might bring.

As already discussed in Chapter 2, the decision by many blacks to support the war was based on the hope that such direct action would increase their political bargaining power and also render the government more sympathetic to black political aspirations.

This hope for some sort of tangible recognition of their service can be seen in interviews in July 1917 by the Governor-General of South Africa, Lord Buxton, with SANLC veterans recently returned to South Africa at the expiry of their contracts. In the words of an interpreter, speaking on behalf of six men interviewed by Lord Buxton, the men considered it a great privilege to have been called on by the king to help: 'It is like a boy being called on by his father to help him make a cattle kraal. They wanted the King to know that they rejoiced to help him, and they were glad of his condescension in asking them. After the war our names will appear in history'.[8]

During the course of the war, statements by international statesmen and other dignitaries heightened black expectations. On 10 July 1917, for example, King George V inspected and addressed members of the SANLC at Abbeville in France (Fig 12.1). For many of the members of the corps, it was an unforgettable experience to see the King, the supreme symbol of British imperial power, in person. But what made this event even more memorable was his address, in which he not only praised them for their labour but also assured them, 'You are also part of my great armies fighting for the liberty and freedom of my subjects of all races and creeds throughout the empire'. The implications seemed clear.[9] The King was reminded of this apparent promise and of the contribution of black South Africans to the war effort in a petition presented to him by a South African Native National Congress delegation sent to England in 1919 to argue for black political representation in South Africa.[10]

David Lloyd George, the British Prime Minister, and Woodrow Wilson, the American President, expounded the idea, from 1918 onwards, that allowance should be made in the post-war dispensation for the self-determination of smaller and oppressed nations.[11] It soon became clear, however, that these statements applied to European nations and not to those striving for self-determination within Britain's Empire and Dominions.

Fig 12.1 SANLC members meeting King George V at Abbeville, France, July 1917.
[© National Library of Scotland]

Of more direct South African import were the words of Governor-General Buxton who, when he addressed a mass meeting of black South Africans during the peace celebrations in December 1918, declared: 'the war has proved to you that your loyalty was well placed, and I can assure that it will not be forgotten'.[12]

The response from black political leaders was unequivocal. Thomas Levi Mvabaza, newspaper editor and founding member of the SANNC, writing in *Abantu-Batho* in April 1918 was clear in what he expected: 'In consideration of the sacrifices the Bantu have made during the war which we are continually being told is for democracy and freedom, the British and the white people of this land should redress our grievances and give the freedom for which we lost thousands of men in this struggle'. Writing in the same newspaper earlier that year, one of its editors, Daniel Letanka, was equally uncompromising: 'We expect to be rewarded for our work after the war when prizes are distributed to the brave who were in battle'.[13]

The South African Government had no intention of remembering the black role in the conflict or of altering the political status quo, however, and 'considered it politically imprudent to acknowledge publicly that whites had required the services of blacks during war-time'.[14] Like the black political leaders, the Government was aware that official acknowledgement that the British Empire had required the help of the black majority in

South Africa to win the war would be a victory for black politics in South Africa. This would have greatly strengthened the demands of black people for a just political dispensation. From the earliest discussions around possible black involvement in the war, the South African Government had thus been concerned that the role of blacks in the war effort should be played down as far as possible. After the war, it chose to neutralise the contribution of black South Africans by offering no acknowledgment of it. Thus, while white South Africans commemorated and memorialised their role in the conflict – for example, the defence of Delville Wood by the South African Brigade in July 1916 – an official policy of stony silence descended on the memory of the SANLC.

Within the communities from which the victims of the *Mendi* came, however, annual commemorations of the event took root and spread. As black political rights were increasingly eroded during the four decades after the war, these commemorations became a focus for political activism and a rallying point for South Africa's growing black nationalist movement.

Home again

What of the experience of the members of the SANLC as they returned home? For most, life simply resumed its former pattern – a daily struggle to survive in a country where civil liberties and economic opportunities for the black majority were being constantly eroded. Many were probably treated as local heroes, their experiences and return to be wondered at by those they had left behind. Stimela Jason Jingoes was met by whooping and incredulity on his return from France, the response from his community reflecting the belief the 'no black person could cross the sea and return'.[15] All black members of the SANLC were probably profoundly changed by their service. No matter how circumscribed and constrained their freedom of movement and association while in France, their view of the world and their place in it is likely to have altered fundamentally by the mere fact of their participation in the SANLC. One former member of the corps wrote: 'We were aware, when we returned, that we were different from the other people at home. Our behaviour, as we showed the South Africans, was something more than they expected from a Native, more like what was expected among them of a white man'.[16]

White South Africans must have sensed this change. One white officer reportedly told members of the corps in France: 'When you people get back to SA, don't start thinking that you are whites, just because this place has spoiled you. You are black, and you will stay black'.[17]

The Government offered no pension to the men who returned. The only compensation was for those who had suffered injury or death, to a maximum of £50.[18] Chiefs and headmen deemed to have been unswervingly loyal to the war effort – this loyalty generally measured by the number of SANLC recruits they had provided – were rewarded, however. Rifles were presented at ceremonies at which King George V himself was to have officiated, although this role ultimately fell to local magistrates after the Government was informed that 'His Royal Highness has no intention of visiting the Territories in the near future'.[19]

Thus, although a symbolic gesture was made towards some of those who played a role in recruiting for the SANLC, no benefit or recognition accrued to the men who actually served. Instead, prevailing prejudices seem to have been reinforced. Throughout the life of the corps, Jan Smuts, the Minister of Defence, repeatedly warned against the use of blacks. He feared the results of drilling them and 'teaching them the arts of war, as the Germans were doing', suggesting that 'armies may yet be trained there, which under proper leading might prove a danger to civilization itself'.[20]

The British War Medal

In 1919, George V instituted the British War Medal (Fig 12.2) to mark service during the war by subjects of the Empire and beyond. Approximately 6.5 million of these medals were struck and roughly 110,000 were issued to veterans of the various foreign labour corps.

In a bitterly resented decision, which Gleeson calls 'one of the most unworthy decisions ever taken by the South African authorities regarding the SANLC', the Government decided that it would not award a war service medal to any of the black ex-SANLC members, nor would it put

Fig 12.2 British War Medal (silver).

their names forward to the War Office in London to allow them to receive the British War Medal. This, despite the British authorities having made provision for the award and the South African authorities having originally agreed to the inclusion of the SANLC in the medal rolls.[21]

The original decision to place SANLC members on the medal rolls was taken by Jan Smuts, who had succeeded Louis Botha as Prime Minister, and his Government in March 1921. However, the finalisation of the award was dealt with so ineptly by the Smuts Government that it was still dragging on when, in 1924, a National Party and Labour Party coalition swept Smuts from power. The new, more conservative Cabinet, which was much less inclined to consider the award of these medals, was able to shift the blame for the lack of action around the medal issue to its predecessor, informing the Governor-General that 'The recent government, as a matter of policy, decided not to proceed with the issue of war medals to non-European members of the Coloured and Native Labour Contingents, and subsequently no steps were taken to furnish any general medals rolls'. The new Government then went further, stating that it had decided that it would serve no useful purpose to reverse this decision.[22]

This conscious snub was compounded when black South African members of the SANLC witnessed the corps' white personnel receiving the British War Medal in silver and men from their own battalions, but from Swaziland, Lesotho and Botswana, being nominated for and receiving their bronze medals (Fig 12.3).[23] A further irony was the inclusion in a list of recommendations for additional awards for special service by Colonel Pritchard, Commanding Officer of the SANLC, of the names of 92 black members of the corps. These recommendations resulted in the award of the Meritorious Service Medal to four white and six black NCOs of the SANLC.[24]

In addition to the lack of medals, veterans of the SANLC were denied any gratuities, and promises made during recruiting were not kept. Recruits had been told that they would be relieved of paying poll tax while

Fig 12.3 Medal roll in Public Records Office, London. [© John Gribble]

on service, would be exempted from pass laws and would receive grants of land and cattle. None of this happened. Instead, SANLC members found themselves liable for poll tax for the entire period they had been absent from South Africa.[25]

Together with the medal issue, these broken promises engendered a deep and abiding bitterness in SANLC veterans towards South Africa's minority government. For years after the war, the absence of tangible recognition of their service remained a sore and contested point for members of the SANLC. On the 14 July 1925, for example, at a meeting of the Transkei Territories General Council, a resolution was passed requesting that the medals be given to the SANLC veterans: the request was roundly rejected by the Government.[26] It is not surprising, therefore, that veterans felt misled, misused and discarded. One veteran, A K Xabanisa, said he felt 'just like a stone which after killing a bird, nobody bothers about, nobody cares to see where it falls'.[27]

Although, as described in the introductory chapter, the loss of the *Mendi* and the sacrifice of those who died aboard her are now widely and officially commemorated in South Africa, the iniquities of the SANLC and the shameful post-war treatment of SANLC veterans have, to a large extent, never been properly addressed in South Africa and are still deeply felt by their descendants and communities.

13

The wreck of the *Mendi*: an archaeological insight

Discovery

The wreck of the *Mendi* appears to have lain undiscovered on the seabed for almost 30 years until 1945, when it was located during a hydrographic survey, probably carried out by the Royal Navy using echo sounder equipment.[1] However, it was not recognised. Survey systems of the time were of limited accuracy and the wreck was measured as being only 100ft (30m) long, much smaller than it actually was. As a result, it was identified as a lighter.[2] There is no evidence that it was visited by divers at this time.

Hydrographic survey in the area was primarily concerned with the safety of navigation. Although the wreck was detected in subsequent surveys, it appears to have been regarded as being too deep to pose a danger to passing ships. The *Mendi*'s anonymity was not to last, however.

Martin Woodward (Fig 13.1), a self-taught diver living on the Isle of Wight, had started working as a diver in about 1968. After working for a commercial diving company, he set up his own operation in 1973, using a

Fig 13.1 *Diver and wreck investigator Martin Woodward, seen here wearing Siebe-Gorman diving dress. [© Martin Woodward]*

former trawler. Combining his passion for investigating shipwrecks with a salvage interest in the non-ferrous metals and other valuable materials they contained, he set about investigating shipwrecks off the south coast. Recreational diving was then in its infancy in the UK and there were still many wrecks close to the coast that had not been found, or at least not been identified.

In 1974, Woodward was investigating wrecks south of the Isle of Wight, locating them using a magnetometer.[3] The wreck of the *Mendi* lay within his search area. Diving the charted position of what he thought would be a lighter, he instead found himself exploring the remains of a large steel ship. At a depth of almost 40m, little natural light penetrated from the surface and the water was also cloudy from silt and other fine sediments carried in the current or disturbed by his movement. Nevertheless, he was able to see that the wreck of the vessel was sitting on its bottom and leaning over to starboard, so that the port side was upstanding several metres and the starboard side was almost level with the seabed for most of its length. The superstructure had collapsed but there was still deck planking in place and the bow and stern of the ship were quite recognisable, the former being a little better preserved than the latter. He saw two pairs of boilers and, aft of these, an engine, which was on its side and slightly inverted. He was impressed by the quality of the ship's fittings, which seemed to him to be better quality than those that he observed in the tramp ships he usually dived. It was clearly not a warship, but a deck gun indicated to him that the ship had been lost in wartime.[4]

In that and following dives over a number of years, Martin Woodward recovered a number of artefacts in the hope of identifying the ship. Crucially, he recovered a small white ceramic tableware bowl with the crest of the British & African Steam Navigation Company transfer printed on its base. Subsequent research indicated that the *Mendi* was the only B&ASNC ship lost in the area. As he had established that the wreck was the right size and was clearly a steamship, with boilers and engines in the positions expected, he eventually realised that it could only be the *Mendi*.

Woodward continued to dive the wreck over the next few years. His interest was intensified when he learnt about its unusual significance from the Elder Dempster researcher and archivist Jim Cowden. The artefacts that he recovered from the wreck included the bridge telegraph (Fig 13.2) made by Chadburns of Liverpool and the pedestal mount, axle and boss of the ship's wheel (Fig 13.3), both found among what he plausibly interpreted as the remains of the navigating bridge on the seabed next to the starboard side of the ship. Also found were a number of square and arched brass windows and brass portholes, all probably from the collapsed superstructure, together with more crockery with the B&ASNC crest (Fig 13.4) and a small silver or silver-plated platter found by another diver.[5]

Fig 13.2 The Mendi's *bridge telegraph. The face is not original and the telegraph position is not as found. The original face, probably made out of thin metal plate, had corroded away and a similar replacement was installed after recovery. Telegraphs were used to transmit orders from the navigating bridge to the engine room. The Liverpool firm of Chadburns is one of the most famous telegraph makers and their telegraphs are commonly found on wrecks of this period. [© Wessex Archaeology]*

Fig 13.3 The remains of the Mendi's *steering wheel. When found, all that remained of the wooden parts of the wheel were the stubs of the spokes. [© Wessex Archaeology]*

Fig 13.4 The small silver-plated platter recovered from the wreck. Inscribed 'B&ASN CO. LD.' Probably for use by first-class passengers. [© Wessex Archaeology]

Wreck identifications and locations were not always widely publicised and it would seem that many of the divers who visited the wreck in the early 1980s were not initially aware that it was the *Mendi*. Archaeologist and diver John Buglass, who first dived the wreck in 1987, was aware that it had been identified but did not know as what. He therefore carried out his own investigation, recovering finds and coming to the same conclusion as Martin Woodward.[6] He described the wreck as follows:

20/07/87   (Possible) bow area, lots of 18lb cartridges with cordite and primer, recovered 1. Also found a mast. No sign of lights. (Another diver) found 1 porthole.

24/07/87   Good viz, straight onto the boilers and over them on to, poss(ibly), the collapsed bridge area; found a square window then (another diver) found a window and I another...[7]

'Sainsburys'

Although Martin Woodward did not initially publicise the location of his
discovery for fear that it would encourage uncontrolled salvage, awareness
of the wreck gradually grew among the recreational diving community. By
the 1980s, the wreck was becoming regularly dived. At the time, it was a
common and largely uncontroversial practice for divers to recover ship's
fittings and other artefacts from wrecks, and it appears that the *Mendi*
became a popular place to acquire these objects. Its reputation in this
respect grew to such an extent that it earned the nicknames 'Sainsburys'
and 'Safeway' because it was easy for those who dived the wreck to bring
back bags of 'goodies'.[8]

Two published descriptions of the wreck compiled in the late 1980s
or early 1990s have been traced. The first is from an article in *Diver*
magazine, in which the wreck was described as follows:

> She lies north-east to south-west, with her bow still pointing towards
> France. The wreck is on a hard sand seabed and is over twelve metres
> proud. She is breaking up and much of her decking has collapsed, leaving
> her boiler up above the main bulk of the wreckage. In the main tangle there
> are many cases of shells for her gun and other cases of rifle ammunition.
> Most of her portholes are still firmly attached to the plating and are of
> distinctive square shape.[9]

The portholes with the 'distinctive square shape' are likely to be small
rectangular windows or 'lights' from the passenger accommodation on the
poop deck, possibly identical to a rectangular window recovered by divers
(*see* Fig 13.16).[10]

The second description appears to have been written for the magazine
of the Elder Dempster Pensioners' Association, *Elders of Elders*.[11] In it,
the stern of the ship was described as standing over 8m high. Forward of
this, the wreck was described as 'becoming more flattened until there is no
discernible edge to the wreckage and the remains trail off into the seabed'.
The bow is described as being the most intact part of the wreck, although
'canted over to starboard'. The foremast was described as being 'largely
intact', with 4-inch (10cm) shell cases scattered around the forward part
of the wreck. The remains of a head are described, with a row of six or
seven toilet bowls. Galley remains are also described, with two large stacks
of B&ASNC crested soup bowls, together with plain white china. Items of
silver tableware, including cutlery and dishes, are described as having been
recovered.

The wreck continued to be visited by recreational divers into the 21st century. A regional dive guide described it as follows: 'Today the wreck lies in a north-east to south-west direction and is over twelve metres proud. She is breaking up. Much of the decking has collapsed and this leaves the large boiler standing above the main wreckage, in which there are many cases of shells and rifle ammunition. Distinctive square portholes can be seen.'[12]

The wreck was resurveyed in 2002 and 2003 and was recorded as being over 130m long by about 31m wide and as standing up to 7m clear of the seabed.[13] It was wire swept at the same time to confirm its depth.[14]

One diver described his dive on the wreck as follows:

She is quite a large wreck and I went from the prop, along the starboard side, up onto the top of the superstructure ... I remember that she does stand proud of the seabed. There is quite a bit of the side still intact. On top of the vessel, she is quite flat as though she has been cabled (swept); the superstructure is relatively non-existent. There was more than the average amount of spidge,[15] although nothing of value. I remember pieces of blue/white porcelain plate and bits of brass in the superstructure.[16]

Following a visit to the wreck in 2005, another diver described it as being 'somewhat scattered and there are mostly plates rather than upright structure. The boiler area is still intact as is a portion of the bow'[17] An account of the wreck written in 2007 described it as standing up to 8m above the seabed. It was leaning over to starboard. The rudder and propeller were described as being in place, with the emergency steering gear nearby. The bow was described as lying on its starboard side. Amidships, the four boilers were still present, with an engine over on its side aft of them. A break in the hull was described between the boilers and bow, with frames and girders, together with a spread of broken crockery and cutlery at this point. The 4.7-inch gun was still mounted to a teak platform on the stern.[18]

Archaeological survey begins

The slow process of deterioration and collapse described by the divers who visited the site in the three decades after its discovery was confirmed by the first archaeological fieldwork to take place on the site in 2007. Archaeological interest had been aroused by a desk-based study carried out in 2006 on behalf of English Heritage,[19] which was in itself an acknowledgement of growing interest in commemorative activities being carried out by Martin Woodward, South African Government representatives and others. In the summer of 2007, geophysical survey data was collected over the wreck during a short survey (Figs 13.5–13.7). Although very poor weather affected the quality of the data gathered, the results provided the first reasonably clear picture of the *Mendi* since it sank in 1917.

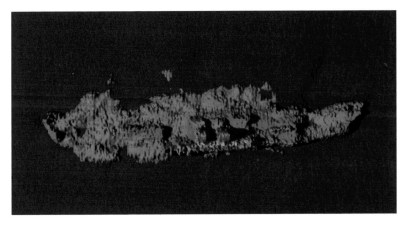

Fig 13.5 Three-dimensional image of the wreck produced using multibeam swath bathymetry. Deeper areas are blue, the highest areas red. West is to the left and the Mendi's *four Scotch boilers can be seen in the middle of the wreck as linear high points. The outline of the* Mendi's *masts on the seabed can also just be seen. [© Wessex Archaeology]*

Fig 13.6 Sidescan sonar image of the wreck. The white area in the centre of the image is the water column directly below the path of the towed sonar, just above the seabed. The white areas above the wreck represent 'acoustic shadows' where the wreck and seabed are masked from the sonar by the highest parts of the wreck. [© Wessex Archaeology]

Fig 13.7 Sidescan sonar image of the wreck. The bow of the ship is on the left. The acoustic shadow areas are shown in black in this image. Rough seas have affected the quality of the survey data and the shape of the wreck has been distorted as a result. [© Wessex Archaeology]

The data confirm that the wreck is 13km south of the Isle of Wight and orientated roughly east-west, with its bow to the west. This was probably the result of the force of the impact, which must have spun the *Mendi* around, as the tide that witnesses said began to flow after the collision did so in an easterly direction.

The sidescan sonar data confirm that the wreck is leaning over to starboard, with much more of the portside hull exposed. The surrounding seabed is fairly flat and featureless, confirming diver descriptions of a hard sand and gravel seabed. There is some indication of outlying debris, possibly objects that became detached as the ship sank.

It is a 55m-long section in the amidships part of the port side of the hull that the data suggest is most upstanding, with a height of over 6m. Both bow and stern can be made out, but they are clearly not as high, being only 1.6m and 2.5m respectively above the seabed, which confirms that they have deteriorated very markedly since the wreck was first discovered. The portside plating is not continuous and the misalignments suggest an ongoing process of collapse. This is particularly clear forward of the boilers along the portside edge of holds 1 and 2, where the data suggest that the hold plating may have fallen inwards towards the centre of the wreck.

Within the hull, all four of the *Mendi*'s cylindrical Scotch boilers are visible, as well as what is probably the engines on their side. The fact that they can clearly be seen confirms that the *Mendi*'s superstructure and decks have collapsed, and extensive debris, particularly on the starboard side, is evident. Both of the ship's intact masts can be seen quite clearly lying partly on the seabed and partly on the wreck, although it is not apparent whether any of the derricks are still attached.

It has been suggested, on the basis of the sidescan sonar data, that the wreck may in fact be lying almost entirely on its starboard side and that what has been interpreted as the port side is in fact the bottom of the ship.[20] However, the diver descriptions consistently refer to it leaning over rather than actually lying on its side.

Recent visitors

The wreck continues to be visited by recreational divers. Although these visits are rarely documented in a way that is readily accessible to researchers, one recent visit has added some detail to knowledge of what is still present on the seabed.

In 2011, Alison Mayor and underwater photographer Martin Davies of Southsea Sub Aqua Club visited the wreck before writing an article on it for the BSAC magazine, *SCUBA*.[21] They described the wreck as lying on its starboard side at an angle of about 45 degrees and with its bows to the west. They observed the port side to be well preserved and standing proud of the seabed by about 6m. Numerous circular holes in the hull plating were observed, although the portholes appeared to have been removed from most.

The decks and superstructure were reported as having collapsed, with their debris lying on the seabed on the starboard side. They encountered four large cylindrical boilers standing up to 5m above the surrounding seabed (Fig 13.8), with some of the associated pipework nearby but damaged. The boilers were toppled over in two pairs. Corrosion has clearly had an impact upon the boiler plating, and holes were spotted in the sides of the boilers.

A large marine steam engine was seen on its side just aft of the boilers, with three pistons and their connecting rods (Fig 13.9). Between the engine and the stern in the area of holds 3 and 4 was what was described as a 'tangled mass' of wreckage, including ribs (ship frames), girders (beams) and wreckage from the superstructure.

Aft of this, the wreckage sloped down towards the stern itself, where the steering quadrant (Fig 13.10), propeller and rudder were seen. The rudder was detached and lying flat on the seabed, although the steering quadrant[22] and propeller were still *in situ*. The ship's 4.7-inch stern gun and its pedestal were also observed to be lying on the seabed, just clear of the stern. Some of the deck planking was attached to the base of the pedestal. Ammunition for this gun was observed nearby.

Along the starboard side, a number of the cargo winches were seen (Fig 13.11), together with both the mainmast and foremast, both lying at a slightly raking angle on the seabed, which suggests that they may have

Fig 13.8 Diver swimming past two of the Mendi's *Scotch boilers. [© Martin Davies]*
Fig 13.9 The Mendi's *engine, lying over on its side. [© Martin Davies]*

broken free of the ship as it struck the seabed. Between the boilers and the bow, a great deal of debris was reported, particularly where the forward superstructure and holds 1 and 2 were. Plates and crockery were found, some of which had the B&ASNC transfer print. There was a break in the ship's structure where Mayor and Davies thought the impact point was.

Fig 13.10 The Mendi's *steering quadrant. [© Martin Davies]*
Fig 13.11 One of the Mendi's *cargo winches. [© Martin Davies]*

Forward of this, the bow was observed in a collapsed condition, lying over on its starboard side and standing just a few metres above the seabed. Mayor and Davies reported the bow as having collapsed in recent years.

Understanding the condition of the wreck

Comparing Mayor and Davies' account with those of early visitors suggests that since the *Mendi* settled on the seabed in 1917, it has endured a process of natural decline. In this it appears to be typical of the many iron and steel wrecks around the British coast that are reaching the centenary of their sinking. Although a few have been salvaged, some have been levelled to the seabed or scattered as hazards to navigation, and some were even depth-charged as suspected U-boats during the Second World War, the principal agent of the gradual collapse and piecemeal disappearance of these wrecks is generally accepted to be saltwater corrosion. This tends to be general to the whole of a wreck, with localised 'hot spots'. By eating away at plate and frame thickness and by loosening joints and rivets, corrosion affects the weight-bearing capacity of the structure of the ship and therefore causes localised collapses that eventually become general. The defences designed into ships do not last long beyond the sinking because paintwork is not renewed and anodes[23] quickly become exhausted.

Unfortunately, and despite growing awareness – since the advent of recreational diving – of the gradual decline of 19th- and 20th-century wrecks, the archaeological response has been slow in coming. The reasons for this are obscure, but perhaps reflect an archaeological preoccupation with periods perceived to be less well documented, as well as, perhaps, a degree of complacency due to the sheer number of relatively intact wrecks that have been recorded. As a result, there has been little monitoring of corrosion and little research into its potentially complex interaction with other agents of change, for example storm waves and suspended sediment carried in tidal currents.

Consequently, it is difficult to assess the impact of corrosion upon the wreck of the *Mendi*, although the limited information retrieved from diver accounts suggests that it has probably been significant. For example, the collapse of the bow onto its side is likely to be at least partly due to the loss of structural integrity that corrosion causes.

Unfortunately, it is also unclear what condition the ship was in when it finally settled on the seabed after sinking. After losing buoyancy, it effectively fell through the water column, bow and starboard first. It then struck a reportedly firm seabed and must have done so hard, with thousands of tons of force. Whether the superstructure collapsed at that point, and was effectively thrown to the starboard side, or whether it collapsed subsequently, remains a mystery. Whether the fractures in the hull that have separated the bow and been seen on the port side occurred as a result of this impact or happened later is also unknown. Likewise, there is little solid information about the impact of human activities upon the wreck. No information exists about the wreck prior to its discovery. Hydrographic surveys have been carried out and the wreck is known to have been wire-swept at least once in 2003 to establish its minimum depth. This practice, although not generally intended to reduce the height of a wreck unless it is considered to be dangerous, can nevertheless be damaging, particularly to wrecks that are already in a weakened condition. In the case of the *Mendi*, although one diver has said that in 2003–4 the top of the wreck was 'quite flat as though she had been cabled',[24] there is no direct evidence that any significant damage was caused by this practice.

From their own descriptions, it is clear that the activities of divers have had an effect upon what remains of the site. It is widely believed, and almost certainly true, that far more has been recovered from the wreck than is currently in the public domain. The initial archaeological study in 2006–7 established that the Receiver of Wreck knew of only 17 individual or groups of objects recovered from the *Mendi*. A number that have recently been donated or loaned for exhibition purposes appear to have been declared to local representatives of the Receiver prior to the centralisation of records in the early 1990s. A number of others are anecdotally known of, including a 'steam chest', or reservoir from the ship's steam machinery, which resides in a private home in Poole, Dorset. But it is likely that significantly more artefacts have been removed from the site than have been declared.

Mendi artefacts

John Buglass's Dive Log for 18 June 1986 reads: 'Joint dive with some people from Chichester branch[25]... The sea bed was 39 metres. Another area was of piles of shell cases – unloaded. I raised one case and two plates, one mug shard.'

The brass shell or cartridge case raised by John Buglass can be seen in Fig 13.12. The case is for a 4.7-inch quick-firing gun, a type typically fitted to defensively armed merchant ships such as the *Mendi*. The markings on the base indicate that it was manufactured in 1897 by the Elswick Ordnance Company and had already been fired once. The case would have been packed with cordite, the low-explosive used as a propellant for the projectile. Its purpose was to protect the cordite during transport and stowage and also to protect the gunners by sealing and preventing the explosive force of the propellant from bursting out of the breach of

0   50   100 mm

Fig 13.12 Brass cartridge case from the Mendi's 4.7-inch gun. [© Wessex Archaeology]

the gun. The projectile can be manufactured attached to the case ('fixed ammunition') or carried and loaded separately ('separate ammunition'). In this case, the cartridge was separate. Although it is not certain that the case was for the *Mendi*'s gun, it seems likely.[26]

The *Mendi*'s gun was manned by Leading Seaman William Carroll and H McDonald. Carroll did not survive the sinking and his body was never found.

The same entry in Buglass's dive log continues 'Wreck is very broken up massive plates and ribs, etc. everywhere. Found one area of piles and piles of plates/soup bowls, white with blue markings and pattern.'

Figure 13.13 shows pieces of ship's crockery recovered by John Buglass and others. They are underglazed transfer-printed earthenwares that include a fragment of the mug or coffee can mentioned above, dishes and a dish fragment. All have the marks of the B&ASNC, the associated African Steam Navigation Company and Elder Dempster on their bases. They were manufactured by Mintons of Stoke-on-Trent, England, and are decorated in the very popular Key Festoon pattern, with a band, swags and diamonds. Though registered in 1868, this design proved to be very popular and was still being manufactured in the early 1900s. It is likely that the officers of the Labour Corps and the ship, and probably also the white NCOs, had their meals and drinks served using this type of tableware, which would ordinarily have been used by paying passengers. The ordinary members of the Corps and of the crew were probably served on plain crockery or other containers.

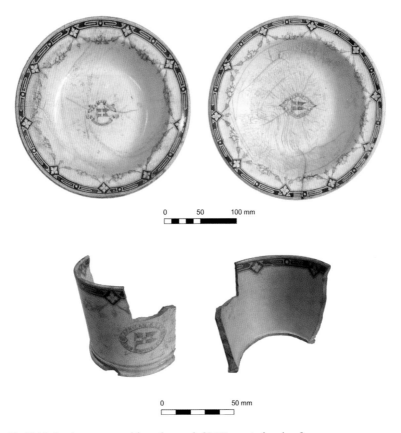

0   50   100 mm

0   50 mm

Fig 13.13 Crockery recovered from the wreck. [© Wessex Archaeology]

As well as the domestic assemblage, the structure of the ship is represented in a number of the finds that have been recovered by divers. Fig 13.14 shows a window from the first-class passenger accommodation. As well as this example, recovered by John Buglass, a number of others were recovered by Martin Woodward.[27] This design of brass sliding window with a curved upper frame and glass and a worm-screw-operated slide can be seen in the ship plans (Fig 13.15) in the port- and starboard-facing bulkheads[28] of the dining room on the poop deck and the music room on the bridge deck above. It can also be seen in photographs of the *Mendi*, particularly of the stern-facing bulkhead of the first-class smoke room, where windows that could be opened would have been particularly necessary to combat the stifling combined effect of cigar and pipe smoke and the African humidity. In the example shown here, the handle of the worm screw is missing.

Fig 13.14 Brass and glass
first-class accommodation
sliding window, inboard side.
[© Wessex Archaeology]

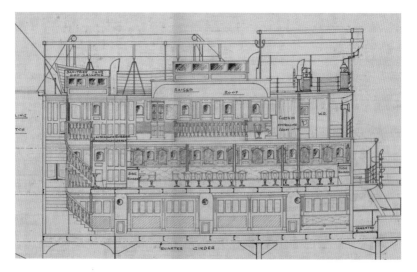

Fig 13.15 Plans of the Mendi, showing the possible original locations of the window shown in
Fig 13.14. [© National Maritime Museum ASAB0109]

Fig 13.16 may be a brass hopper-style window from the forward bulkhead of the first-class dining saloon, as a line of rectangular windows can be seen in that location in photographs of the ship (Fig 13.17 and *see* Fig 7.4). However, these do look somewhat larger than the recovered window.

At least three different types of brass portholes can be seen in photographs of the *Mendi*. Most were simple scuttles with a metal frame attached to a circular opening in the ship's plating and a hinged circular frame with glass that opened inwards and was secured when closed by means of butterfly clips (Fig 13.18). Those portholes in the hull that might compromise the ship's watertightness if broken would be protected inside by a hinged blanking plate called a deadlight. Most would also have an external brow designed to channel water running down the ship away from them, as well as a drip tray inside.

Some were also protected by three vertical bars attached to the outside of the frame, as can be seen in the lower left in Fig 13.19. This would protect them from impact; for example, the portholes along the side of the holds would be barred to protect them from swinging loads during cargo handling. However, the example shown in Fig 13.20 has five external bars, probably to protect compartments in the superstructure that held valuable items. The same type of porthole was fitted to the purser's cabin on the poop deck. This cabin would, of course, have held the ship's safe, which could still be present in the wreck.

0   50   100 mm

Fig 13.16 Rectangular brass and glass window, possibly of the 'hopper' type. [© Wessex Archaeology]

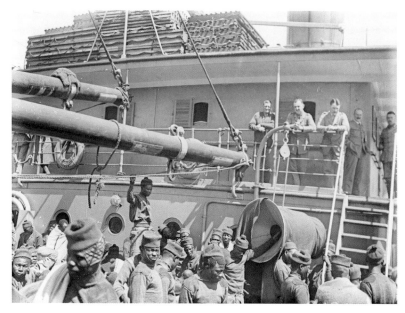

Fig 13.17 Photograph taken from the poop deck looking at the aft end of the superstructure. The circular portholes are for the second-class dining room and saloon. [© Imperial War Museum Q15657]

Fig 13.18 A scuttle still attached to the steel plating of the ship. [© Keith Rimes]

Fig 13.19 *The* Mendi *being boarded in Africa by British officers, prior to its use as a transport for the SANLC. To the right of the general leading the party boarding are the barred portholes of the purser's cabin. [© Imperial War Museum Q015662]*

Fig 13.20 *Brass and glass porthole protected by a set of five bars, possibly from the purser's cabin. [© Wessex Archaeology]*

The *Mendi*'s wider place in the maritime landscape

Acknowledgement of the importance of the *Mendi* came in the form of designation under the Protection of Military Remains Act following the archaeological work carried out in 2006–7. As a Protected Place, the wreck can still be dived, but it cannot be lawfully disturbed, except under licence.

However, while the wreck is undoubtedly of international importance in itself, it also forms part of the much wider maritime archaeological landscape caused by the First World War. In the year that the *Mendi* sank, the war claimed another 1,196 British merchant ships.[29] Of the 2,479 merchant ships lost in the entire war, losses in the English Channel figure disproportionately, reflecting the intensity of the war at sea there. Indeed, the Admiralty's Weekly Reports from Coastal Stations recorded more than 750 ships sunk in the Channel during the war.[30] Records held by the National Record of the Historic Environment (NRHE) suggest that the majority of these are known archaeological sites: there are over 390 known wrecks dating from this period on the seabed. While troopship losses represent just a tiny fraction of the Channel losses and of worldwide losses, they are disproportionately important because of the very high loss of life associated with them. For example, the loss of the French transports *Gallia* and *Athos*, in 1916 and 1917 respectively, resulted in a total loss of life of 2,092. The loss of the *Otranto* in 1917, rammed by another ship and then forced ashore at the Isle of Islay by rough weather, resulted in the loss of approximately 470 American soldiers.[31] The torpedoing and very rapid sinking of the *Royal Edward* off the Greek island of Kandeloussa resulted in the loss of 935 British troops bound for Gallipoli.[32] Australian transports were lost in some numbers: of the 21 sunk, 5 were lost in the English Channel, although they appear to have been working as hospital ships or general transports at the time.[33]

The *Mendi* was not the only loss suffered by labour corps: when the French liner *Athos* sank en route for Marseille from Yokohama, on 17 February 1917, 754 lives were lost, including 543 Chinese Labourers.[34] Danger at sea also continued to haunt the men of the SANLC: on 10 September 1918, the Union Castle line *Galway Castle* left Plymouth bound for Cape Town, with 399 walking wounded from the South African army and SANLC among its passengers. At the time, the ship, which had previously been requisitioned as a troop transport, had been returned to normal Union Castle service. Two days out it was torpedoed. Fortunately, the submarine did not press home the attack and, although the weather was rough, the ship had been sailing in convoy, so the survivors were picked up relatively quickly. Nevertheless, more than 140 men died.[35]

Aside from dealing with Jacobite insurrection, the last 400 years has seen the British fight almost exclusively abroad. The close connection between the soldier and the sea that has resulted is something that has been argued as being peculiarly British, and the British Army has been succinctly described as 'a projectile launched by the fleet'.[36] The importance of troopships such as the *Mendi* to the British Empire's war effort in Europe is therefore hard to understate. All of the troops and labourers used had to go by sea; there simply was no alternative. Without the soldiers and labourers of its Dominions and colonies, it is most unlikely that the war effort on the Western Front could have been sustained, so the humble troopship was therefore every bit as important to the war effort as the most powerful battleship of the Grand Fleet.

14
Conclusion

In the 100 years since the loss of the *Mendi*, the event and the stories associated with it have been commemorated, forgotten and latterly rediscovered by South Africa and the world. The sacrifice of the men who died in the cold waters of the English Channel that February morning in 1917 is now rightly and appropriately marked by memorials across South Africa and in the UK and by annual commemorations in both countries.

Remembrance of the First World War has historically been preoccupied with a 'white' war fought on the Western Front by European and other white troops. The 1914–18 centenary commemorations have provided the opportunity for historians and archaeologists to re-examine this narrative: to highlight the vital role played by non-white troops and non-combatants; to reconsider the crucial role played by merchant shipping in determining the war's outcome; and to explore the potential for archaeology to add not just to our knowledge but also to our commemoration of the war. These strands come together in the story of the *Mendi*. Lying in quiet darkness off the Isle of Wight, its wreck has become a portal into a neglected but important aspect of the First World War: the wartime labour system.

The *Mendi*, like each of the thousands of merchant ships lost between 1914 and 1918, is also part of the bigger picture of the First World War. Without the gallant efforts of their crews in transporting men and materials, that war would have had a very different outcome. Most of these merchant losses were quickly forgotten and are only recently being rediscovered as a result of the efforts of divers and archaeologists. However, there is a very rare group of historic shipwrecks the repercussions of whose loss have instead rippled forward in time to influence later events. The *Mendi* is one of them: a loss that became a symbol in the fight against the inequality and oppression of the apartheid state; a loss that is now an important part of the story of a new 'rainbow nation'.

No one who was aboard the *Mendi* or who served in the SANLC is alive today, nor is any other veteran of the other foreign labour corps. The First World War has passed from memory and into history, and the direct, personal link the world once had with that awful conflict has been severed. Access to the war now is through documents, objects and archaeological sites. Part of the value of sites like the *Mendi* is thus the physical link they provide with the past.

While much of this book has explored the link that the *Mendi* provides with the First World War labour system, the *Mendi* is also a reminder of just how multi-layered and diverse the meaning and significance of shipwreck sites can be. As well as its importance to the people and Government of South Africa, both as a symbol and as a war grave, it is now being used in Britain to promote ideas of equality within society, for example by former Prime Minister David Cameron, in a speech delivered at the Imperial War Museum in 2012.[1]

It is a period of history through which the origins of a number of very significant advances can be traced: the extraordinary bravery of Edith Cavell, whose actions gained such widespread admiration, played an important part in advancing the emancipation of women; and the loss of the troopship SS *Mendi* in February 1917 and the death of the first black British army officer, Walter Tull, in March 1918 are not just commemorated as tragic moments, but also seen as marking the beginnings of ethnic minorities getting the recognition, respect and equality they deserve.

To the people of England, the *Mendi* is part of their underwater heritage, one of the richest in the world, and it is one of the few wrecks considered sufficiently important to be formally protected by law. In Scotland, it provides a tangible link with a once world-leading shipbuilding industry. For the people of Liverpool, it is a physical link with a great maritime heritage, with that city's controversial colonial past and with one of the city's famous shipping lines. It helps unlock aspects of the First World War that have been sadly overlooked, and the diversity of its crew reminds us of that other great international labour system of the war, the merchant navy. The *Mendi*, of course, is not without significance to avocational divers: knowledge of the site still largely relies upon their efforts.

The *Mendi* is an example to both archaeologists and those charged with safeguarding the maritime heritage of the UK that the value of shipwrecks lies in more than what their surviving fabric can tell us about how the ship was built, operated and who sailed on it. It demonstrates that value can also be wider than the narrow 'significance' criteria that underpin how historic shipwrecks are managed under national legislation and international treaty: it lies in the people they carried; in what happened after the ship was lost as well as before; in what they mean to contemporary society. Whereas a South African descendant may see the *Mendi* purely as a war grave, a Glaswegian may see its value principally in terms of their city's maritime heritage and a diver may see the site, respectfully, in terms of a recreational activity. Understanding the value of a shipwreck therefore requires archaeologists and policy makers to understand who they are valuing it for and to engage in dialogue with them.

This study was written at a time when the people of the UK were deciding whether to redraw their relationship with the other countries of the European Union. The *Mendi* is therefore a timely reminder that the UK's maritime heritage is a shared international heritage. Ships and people of many places and nations were lost in English waters during the First World War and, as this study has hopefully demonstrated, what might seem just an ordinary shipwreck in one place can have a value that renders it extraordinary elsewhere. In an era in which the future of the union that forms the UK is very much a live issue, it is also a reminder that the maritime heritage in England is shared by Scotland, Wales and Northern Ireland – and indeed other nations.

For a site with such international resonance, it is perhaps surprising that the wreck has not been more thoroughly explored by archaeologists. The most recent geophysical survey was in 2007 and, although many divers have visited it, the site has never been systematically surveyed and recorded by divers. Although a good deal is known about the history of the *Mendi* and about the multiple meanings that attach themselves to the ship, far less is known about the wreck itself. For example, no information exists about artefacts and other material evidence for the SANLC, which it is thought probably lies within its remains. Neither is it known whether human remains are present, although this seems likely.

The reason for this lack of investigation lies partly in lack of opportunity, which is in turn linked to lack of funding for archaeology on the seabed. It lies also in a traditional lack of attention given to 20th-century heritage on the seabed by archaeologists and curators, although this has been changing in recent years as interest in the 1914–18 commemorations has increased, and as a result of various Historic England and other heritage initiatives.

As a result of the lack of archaeological investigation, little is known about how the wreck site is changing over time. While in use, ships like the *Mendi* were protected from saltwater corrosion by the regular renewal of layers of paint and anodes. After they were lost, this protection was also lost. As a result, they are collapsing due to corrosion, exacerbated by other natural processes and human activity. A substantial amount survives, but it is a diminishing asset and it is therefore important that archaeological recording should be carried out before it is too late.

The *We Die Like Brothers* exhibition at Delville Wood forms part of the centenary commemorations of the loss of the *Mendi* taking place in both South Africa and the UK. The presentation by the South African Government of *Mendi* Medals to descendants of SANLC men as part of this commemoration will continue the process of righting the wrongs of the past. It will also highlight the importance of a shipwreck that now stands for equality and a shared heritage in both South Africa and the UK.

Notes

Chapter 1

1   While the authors consider all who live, or have lived, in South Africa, and who identify with the country, to be Africans, this is a story that, at its heart, is about race and that is defined by the application of artificial classifications of people based on the colour of their skin. It is also a story told from the South African present, where historical imperatives still impose the use of the terms black, white and coloured in South Africa's everyday life. The authors acknowledge that these terms may be deemed offensive but, given the historical context, have no other way of telling the story other than making use of such designations. For clarity, 'black' refers to Bantu-speaking people of Africa, 'white' describes people of European descent, while 'coloured', in the South African context, refers to people of mixed descent. Where other derogatory racial terms are used in the source documents quoted in the text, these terms have been retained. Their use in no way reflects the personal views of the authors or the publisher.

Chapter 2

1   Hacker, 28; Starling and Lee, 84. Military fatigue duty is the labour assigned to military men that does not require the use of arms (*see* Farrow, 623).
2   Due to their good pay and comfortable and comparatively safe service conditions, the ASC were not regarded by the infantry as proper soldiers. This gave rise to a number of uncomplimentary nicknames, including Aunt Sally's Cavalry, the Army Safety Corps and Ally Sloper's Cavalry, after Ally Sloper, a popular British comic character who was an archetypal lazy schemer. When the ASC acquired their well-earned 'Royal' prefix in 1918, to become the RASC, their nickname became 'Run Away, Someone's Coming'.
3   Hacker, 28.
4   Starling and Lee, 77.
5   For a discussion about this popular myth *see* Hallifax, 103–21.
6   Starling and Lee, 78.
7   Hacker, 27.
8   The Western Front Association, 'The British pioneer battalions and labour corps on the Western Front'. Available online at www.westernfrontassociation. com/the-great-war/great-war-on-land/general-interest/810-labour-corps-pionners.html#sthash. uv13BVQq.dpbs (accessed 27 July 2016).
9   Starling and Lee, 78–9.
10 Starling and Lee, 81–2.
11 The Long, Long Trail, 'The labour corps of 1917–1918', 1996. Available online at www.longlongtrail.co.uk/army/regiments-and-corps/the-labour-corps-of-1917-1918/ (accessed 27 July 2016).
12 *See* Starling and Lee, 92, for details of this corps.
13 According to Hacker, 29, Indian troops made up a quarter of the British army on the Western Front during the winter of 1914–15.

14 Hacker, 29.

15 Starling and Lee, 95.

16 Hacker, 27.

17 Starling and Lee, 95–6.

18 Starling and Lee, 100.

19 Gleeson, 30. *See also* Starling and Lee, which provides the most comprehensive study of the British wartime labour apparatus to date.

20 Hacker, 27.

21 Starling and Lee, 100.

22 Starling and Lee, 101.

23 Starling and Lee, 100–1. *See* Young for a detailed history of the Army Service Corps.

24 Starling and Lee, 102.

25 Gleeson, 30.

26 Starling and Lee, 102; Hacker, 32.

27 Starling and Lee, 104 and 105.

28 Ibid; *see also* Putkowski, 26–7.

29 Fawcett, 34.

30 Starling and Lee, 125.

31 Grundlingh 1987, 112–13; Starling and Lee, 125.

32 Modern Qingdao in eastern Shandong Province.

33 Xu Guoqi, 13.

34 Hacker, 33.

35 Xu Guoqi, 16–17.

36 Ibid.

37 The National Archives, WO 106/33, Contract for Chinese labourers for France.

38 Ibid.

39 Fawcett, 37.

40 Xu Guoqi, 23–7.

41 Xu Guoqi, 27.

42 Starling and Lee, 96.

43 Modern Weihai in China's Shandong Province.

44 Fawcett, 40; Starling and Lee, 298; *see also* Klein for a first-hand account of the author's experiences as an officer in the Chinese Labour Corps, including their travel to and across Canada in Part II of his book.

45 Xu Guoqi, 18.

46 Hacker, 33.

47 Fawcett; Commonwealth War Graves Commission, 'The Chinese Labour Corps at the Western Front', nd. Available online at www.skycitygallery.com/japan/wwi_chinese_1.pdf (accessed 27 July 2016).

48 Starling and Lee, 96.

49 Starling and Lee, 270.

50 Hacker, 32; Starling and Lee, 270; *See also* Killingray 1989, 485.

51 Elgood, 314; Putkowski, 29.

52 Hacker, 33.

53 Ibid.

54 *Fellah* was term for a peasant, farmer or agricultural labourer in the Middle East and North Africa. *Fellahin* is the plural.

55 Starling and Lee, 273.

56 Starling and Lee, 275.

57 Starling and Lee, 276.

58 Putkowski, 29–30; Starling and Lee, 277.

59 The National Archives, WO 107/37, Report on the work of labour with the BEF during the war, Cape Boys Labour Battalion; Gleeson, 55; Hacker, 31.

60 Starling and Lee, 161–95.

61 Ibid.

62 Killingray 1989, 483–501; Savage and Forbes Munro, 313–432.

63 Killingray 1989, 483.

64 Walton, 13.

Chapter 3

1 Marti; Truman.

2 Worden, 33–7.

3 Mohlamme, 2; Clothier, 5; Grundlingh 1987, 7.

4 Nasson 2014, 20–1.

5 Nasson 2014, 15–27.

6 Clothier, 6.

7 Gleeson, 10.

8 Truman.

9 Grundlingh 1987, 21.

10 *See* Swart for an exploration of the causes of the Afrikaner Rebellion.

11 Grundlingh 1987, 21–2.

12 Nasson 2014, 15–27; Gleeson, 10.

13 Paterson, 2; *see also* Collyer 1937 for a detailed account of the Union's military campaign in German South-West Africa.

14 Grundlingh 1987, 5; Warwick, 4.

15 Grundlingh 1987, 5.

16 Walton, 22.

17 Worden, 54.

18 Mkhize, 17.

19 Walton, 22.

20 Clothier, 10; Grundlingh 1987, 39; Mohlamme, 2.

21 National Archives (Pretoria), GNLB 187/1217/14/D110.

22 Clothier, 11; Grundlingh 1987, 39.

23 Grundlingh 1987, 13.

24 Grundlingh 1987, 3.

25 Cape Archives, CMT 3/929 778/2, Telegram to NATLAB from Mt Fletcher and Umtata (11 December 1916); Walton, 22; Grundlingh 1987, 15–19.

26 Clothier, 11.

27 Plaatje, 281.

28 Grundlingh 1987, 37.

29 Starling and Lee, 225; Walton, 24.

30 The National Archives, CO 537/604/46680, Report regarding the raising and training of native troops.

31 Gleeson, 9.

32 Grundlingh 1987, 38.

33 *See* Mostert.

34 Gleeson, 12.

35 Plaatje, 282–3.

36 Grundlingh 1987, 39.

37 Grundlingh 1987, 40.

38 Grundlingh 1987, 28.

39 Clothier, 11.

Chapter 4

1 Grundlingh 1987, 40.

2 Plaatje, 268.

3 Gleeson, 14.

4 Ibid.

5 Gleeson, 13; Nasson 2007, 65.

6 Willan, 64.

7 Gleeson, 15.

8 Gleeson, 14–15; Nasson 2007, 65.

9 Grundlingh 1987, 87.

10 Collyer 1937.

11 Killingray 2001, 425–43. *See also* Collyer 1939 and Samson for detailed accounts of the East African campaign.

12 Nasson 2007, 96; Gleeson, 17.

13 Gleeson, 17–18; Nasson 2007, 96.

14 Gleeson, 19.

15 Ibid.

16 Grundlingh 1987, 87; Nasson 2007, 106.

17 Gleeson, 18.

18 Grundlingh 1987, 88.

19 Grundlingh 1987, 89.

20 Grundlingh 1987, 91.

21 Killingray 1989, 485.

22 Starling and Lee, 192.

23 Killingray 1989, 485; Killingray 2001, 427.

24 Plaatje, 267.

25 Grundlingh 1987, 86.

Chapter 5

1 Starling and Lee, 223.

2 Willan, 64.

3 Grundlingh 1987, 41.

4 Grundlingh 1987, 42.

5 The National Archives, LAB 2/169, Telegram from Governor-General of the Union of South Africa to the Secretary of State for the Colonies, received 4.38 pm, 11 April 1916.

6 Starling and Lee, 223.

7 Grundlingh 1987, 42.

8 Starling and Lee, 223.

9 Gleeson, 13; Nasson 2007, 24.

10 Willan, 64.

11 The National Archives, CO 2213, Colonial Office, supply of colonial troops and coloured labour, January 1917.

12 The National Archives, WO 107/37, Appendix F: History of the SANLC; CO 323/757/6, Supply of 'coloured troops' and 'coloured labour': reports from individual colonies (December 1916 – March 1917), 118–22.

13 Turrell, 70–1.

14 Willan, 71.

15 Ibid.

16 Ibid.
17 Nasson 2007, 162.
18 Gleeson, 25.
19 Nasson 2004, 61.
20 Willan, 66–7; Nasson 2007, 162.
21 Cape Archives CMT 3/926 778/2, SANLC: Discontinuance of recruiting (17 March 1917).
22 Cape Archives 1/KNT 22 10/1, Circular no. 11 of 1917: Copy of letter from Councillor H M Tyali of Tsolo who accompanied the first NLC to France (28 May 1917).
23 Nasson 2007, 163–4.
24 Peregrino.
25 Clothier, 19.
26 Cape Archives CMT 3/925 778/2, Chief Magistrate Umtata meeting with Chief Mangala and other chiefs of Western Pondoland (10 November 1916).
27 Cape Archives CMT 3/925 778/2, A K Xabanisa to Chief Magistrate Umtata (28 December 1917).
28 Grundlingh 1987, 75; Gleeson, 26.
29 'Builders of Botswana', *Botswana Daily News*, 5 July 2002, available online at http://www.olddailynews.gov.bw/cgi-bin/news.cgi?d=20020705 (accessed 9 August 2016), cited in Wessex Archaeology 2007.
30 The National Archives, WO 329/2359, South African Native Labour Corps: medal rolls COL/185A; WO 329/2368, South African Native Labour Corps (Bechuanaland): medal rolls COL/185A3; WO 329/2372, South African Native Labour Corps (Basutoland): medal rolls COL/185A2.
31 Nasson 2007, 164.
32 Grundlingh 1982, 3.
33 Grundy, 55; Nasson 2007, 163.
34 Nasson 2007, 165.
35 Grundlingh 1982, 3; Nasson 2004, 61–2; Grundy, 55.
36 Gleeson, 27; *see also* Stuart.
37 National Archives (Pretoria), GNLB 192 1329/14/D48, Proceedings of meeting held at Ebenezer Hall (October 1916).
38 Willan, 67; Grundlingh 1987, 67–8.
38 Nasson 2007, 163.
40 Cape Archives, CMT 3/925 778/2, NATLAB to TEMBU (25 July 1917).
41 Ibid.
42 Cape Archives 1/KNT 22 10/1, Circular 19 of 1917: Office of the Chief Magistrate of the Transkeian Territories, Umtata (14 July 1917); Grundlingh 2014, 47.
43 Cape Archives 1/KNT 22 10/1, Circular 19 of 1917, Office of the Chief Magistrate of the Transkeian Territories, Umtata (14 July 1917).
44 Cape Archives CMT 3/925 778/2, Testimony of Xabanisa, Witbooi and Tebenga re experiences of being with the SANLC in France (October 1917).
45 Cape Archives CMT 3/930 778/2 Pamphlet: 'British Africans in Europe and the Work of the Welfare Committee published by the Committee for the Welfare of Africans in Europe' (22 June 1917).
46 Nasson 2007, 163, quoting Buxton, 288.
47 Walton, 33.
48 Gleeson, 29–30; Walton, 26.
49 Ibid; Gleeson, 26.
50 Clothier, 15.
51 The National Archives, WO 107/37, Appendix G: Notes for officer of labour corps SANLC, report on the work of labour with the BEF during the war: South African Native Labour Contingent; Starling and Lee, 225.
52 National Archives (Pretoria), DC 768 (GP 2) D/5A/1997/3199 *Rand Daily Mail* article (18 September 1916).
53 Clothier, 12.
54 Cape Archives, CMT 3/930 778/2 Pamphlet: 'British Africans in Europe and the work of the Welfare Committee', published by the Committee for the Welfare of Africans in Europe (22 June 1917).
55 Grundlingh 1987, 99–100.

56 Grundlingh 1982, 3.
57 Grundlingh 1987, 102–3.
58 Grundlingh 1987, 103.
59 Many white South Africans referred to all black men as boys.
60 Grundlingh 2014, 81.

Chapter 6

1 Cape Archives, CMT 3/930 778/2 Pamphlet: 'British Africans in Europe and the work of the Welfare Committee', published by the Committee for the Welfare of Africans in Europe.
2 Starling and Lee, 98.
3 National Archives (Pretoria), GG 673 9/93/132, Letter: Prime Minister Botha to Governor-General Buxton (9 February 1917).
4 Ibid.
5 Ibid.
6 The National Archives, MT 23/630, Telegram from SNO Simonstown to Admiralty (19 September 1916).
7 South African National Defence Force Archive (Pretoria), WW1 ISD 24, Letter: HRM Bourne to Colonel Stanford, Union Department of Defence, Treatment of South African soldiers on return to South Africa after discharge in England (1 July 1918).
8 Starling and Lee, 228–9; Walton, 39.
9 Starling and Lee, 98.
10 National Archives (Pretoria), GG 670 9/93/56, War Office report on the SANLC.
11 Nasson 2007, 167; Grundlingh 2014, 73.
12 Walton, 55.
13 Nasson 2007, 166–7.
14 Nissen huts were prefabricated, tunnel-shaped huts made of curved corrugated iron, designed during the First World War by Major Peter Nissen.
15 The National Archives, WO 107/37, Appendix G: Notes for officer of labour corps SANLC, report on the work of labour with the BEF during the war:

South African Native Labour Contingent.
16 Ibid.
17 Nasson 2007, 166.
18 Grundlingh 2014, 84–5.
19 The National Archives, WO 107/37, Appendix G: Notes for officer of labour corps SANLC, report on the work of labour with the BEF during the war: South African Native Labour Contingent.
20 National Archives (Pretoria), GG 673 9/93/132, Extracts from letters received from certain officers of the SANLC.
21 National Archives (Pretoria), GG 670 9/93/56, Letter to Secretary of Native Affairs from G A Godley, Officer Commanding SANLC (8 December 1917).
22 Cape Archives, CMT 3/930 778/2, Pamphlet: 'British Africans in Europe and the work of the Welfare Committee' published by the Committee for the Welfare of Africans in Europe.
23 Gleeson, 30.
24 Ibid.
25 The National Archives, WO 107/37, Appendix G: Notes for officer of labour corps SANLC, report on the work of labour with the BEF during the war: South African Native Labour Contingent; Grundlingh 1987, 98.
26 Cape Archives, CMT 3/930 778/2 Pamphlet: 'British Africans in Europe and the work of the Welfare Committee', published by the Committee for the Welfare of Africans in Europe.
27 *The Cape Times Annual 1919* ('The SA Native Labour Contingent'), cited in Grundlingh 2014, 86.
28 National Archives (Pretoria), GG 670 9/93/56, Pritchard's report on the SANLC (6 October 1916).
29 Cape Archives, CMT 3/930 778/2, Letter from E Mbelu to 'My dear priest' from Havre, France (25 June 1917).

30 Cape Archives, 1/KNT 22 10/1 D, Circular of letter from AK Xabanisa to Mag, Umtata (25 May 1917).

31 Grundlingh 2014, 86.

32 Grundlingh 1987, 108.

33 Grundlingh 1987, 109.

34 Ibid.

35 Now known as silicosis, a lung disease formerly common among miners caused by the inhalation of silica dust.

36 Cape Archives, CMT 3/929 778/2, Telegram from ONC: Medical examination of recruits to all MAG (5 December 1916); CMT 3/930 778/2d, NA to all RM re the scale of rations at Rosebank depot (4 May 1917).

37 That portion of South Africa's inland plateau that has an altitude above 1,500m.

38 South African National Defence Force Archive (Pretoria), DC 768 (GP 2), D100/1997/9199, Minute 1514 on the question of employing South African native labour in the northern part of France (18 October 1916).

39 The National Archives, WO 95/4115, Lines of communication troops, Native Labour Stationary Hospital.

40 National Archives (Pretoria), GG 670 9/93/56, Report on the health of the SANLC at Rouen (4 October 1918).

41 Hacker, 33.

42 South African National Defence Force Archive, SANLC Box 3, SANLC nominal rolls.

43 The National Archives, WO 95/4115, War Diary, 1st Army, C Company, 2nd Battalion SANLC. *See* B Company War Diary below for further detail of Private Samuel Lekuba.

44 The National Archives, WO 95/4115, War Diary, 1st Army, B Company, 2nd Battalion SANLC.

45 The SANLC member killed was Private Samuel Lekuba (Service No. 4053), from Mashashane's location, Pietersburg in the former Transvaal. *See* http://www.cwgc.org/find-war-dead/casualty/186687/ LEKUBA,%20S (accessed 26 July

2016) for details of his grave in Aveluy Communal Cemetery.

46 The National Archives, WO 95/4115, War Diary, 1st Army, B Company, 2nd Battalion SANLC.

47 A heavy German field howitzer.

48 National Archives (Pretoria), NTS 9107 16/363, Letter to Dower, 11 August 1917.

49 Cape Archives, CMT 3/925 778/2, Magistrate Matatiele from Lonsdale. Query: are SANLC to be employed as anything other than dock workers? (23 November 1916).

50 Ibid.

51 The National Archives, WO 107/37, History of the SANLC.

52 The National Archives, WO 95/4115, Report on the SANLC.

53 Ibid.

54 National Archives (Pretoria), GG 9/93/56, War Office report on the SANLC.

Chapter 7

1 Slaven, 156.

2 Slaven, 154.

3 Glasgow University Archive Services, Alexander Stephen & Sons Ltd, 1 September 1857, UGD 4/18/7.

4 Greenway.

5 Grace's Guide, chapter 9.

6 The National Archives, BT 110/364, Registry of shipping and seamen: transcripts and transactions, series IV.

7 Griffiths, 108–9.

8 The National Archives, BT 165/308, Extracted ships' logs: Mendi official number 120875, 22 June 1907–9, August 1907, 9 November 1907–8, December 1907.

9 The National Archives, BT 110/364, Registry of shipping and seamen: transcripts and transactions, series IV.

10 *See* Lugard.

11 Havinden and Meredith, 93–4, 98.

12 Ibid.

13 The National Archives, BT 26/257–
626, Inward passenger lists of Port of
Liverpool.

14 Havinden and Meredith, 93–4, 117.

Chapter 8

1 Possibly recorded and signed as
'Hangaard' in the crew list, but referred
to as Hougaard in the report of the
Court of Inquiry into the loss.

2 Original letter, MacTavish family
archive.

3 Ibid.

4 Clothier, 24–5.

5 Noord-Hollands Archief:
3061(Zandvort)/1327.

6 *The Times* (SA), 22 February 2016,
10–11.

7 Clothier, 44.

8 Wessex Archaeology 2007, 8.

9 Clothier, 50.

10 Clothier, 27.

11 Elder Dempster.

12 The National Archives, BT 99/3345,
Registry of shipping and seamen:
Agreements and crew lists, series II,
Mendi, official no. 120875.

13 Original letter, MacTavish family
archive.

14 The National Archives, ADM 37/360,
Admiralty: Ships' musters (series II).

15 The National Archives, MT9/1115,
Brisk radio log.

16 The National Archives, MT9/1115,
Affidavit of L E Hertslet.

17 The National Archives, MT9/1115,
Affidavit of H L J van Vuren.

18 Clothier, 56.

19 The National Archives, MT9/1115,
Report of Lt Commander Algernon
Lyons.

20 *Cape Times*, 8 February 1947, np.

21 Clothier, 59.

22 Clothier, 62.

23 Clothier, 60.

24 Clothier, 63.

25 The National Archives, MT9/1115,
Affidavit of H L J van Vuren.

26 The National Archives, MT9/1115,
Report of Lt Commander Algernon
Lyons.

27 Ibid.

28 Verbal evidence given to the Court of
Inquiry, quoted in Clothier, 69.

29 Clothier, 69.

30 The National Archives, MT9/1115,
Brisk radio log.

31 Clothier, 71.

32 Clothier, 68, quoting Kenneth Tshite.

Chapter 9

1 Clothier, 74.

2 Clothier, 75.

3 Noord-Hollands Archief:
3061(Zandvort)/1327.

4 Commonwealth War Graves
commission, available online at
http://www.cwgc.org (accessed
27 July 2016).

5 *The Times*, 10 March 1917.

6 Original letter, MacTavish family
archive.

7 Original scroll, MacTavish family
archive.

8 *The Times* (SA), 23 February 2016,
10–11.

9 The National Archives, MT 9/1115,
M32925, letters dated 18 July 1917.

10 The National Archives, MT 9/1115,
'Report of Court'. Other unreferenced
quotations in this chapter also come
from this report of the Inquiry.

11 The National Archives, BT 122/20,
Registry of shipping and seamen:
registers of certificates of competency,
masters and mates, foreign trade,
recorded service: 1877–96 certificate
numbers: 17000–17999, master's
certificate 017169.

12 Lloyd's Captains Registers, MSS 18,
567–711.

13 The National Archives, MT9/1115,
M35117, 11 August 1917.

14 Clothier, 90.

15 *The Times*, 2 August 1917.

16 Ibid.

17 Clothier, 185.

18 The National Archives, MT9/1115, M351117, handwritten note, 15 August 1917.
19 *Brisk's* radio log suggests that over two hours after the collision, the *Darro's* radio operator was still sending to the bridge for information about the damage so that he could tell the *Brisk*.
20 The National Archives, HC 27/165, Limitation of liability. The Royal Mail Steam Packet Co. vs Owners of *Mendi*.
21 Clothier, 171.
22 The National Archives, HCA 20/1536, Affidavit of Ellen Raine. Those effects provide us with an interesting picture of the personal possessions of a young merchant service officer. Raine had a substantial number of books because he was studying for his master's certificate:

> Sextant £20, 10 white duck suits £10, 6 white linen suits £1.10s, 4 woollen shirts £1, 4 sets singlets and pants £1.10s, 2 pyjama suits 10s, boots and slippers £2.5s, raincoat £2.10s, great coat £4, patrol suit £2, uniform £5, 1 suit (mufti) £3, gold watch and chain £10, binoculars £7, 2 Portmanteaux and 1 Saratoga Trunk £5, books (navigation text books, etc) £10. Total £85.5s (equivalent to roughly £4,250 today).

23 The National Archives, HCA 20/1536, Affidavit of Jennie Foster.
24 The National Archives, MT9/1115, Affidavit of H L J van Vuren.
25 The National Archives, MT9/1115, Wrecks: *Mendi*.
26 Clothier, 54.
27 Clothier, 56.
28 The National Archives, MT9/1115, Affidavit of L E Hertslet.
29 Clothier, 84.
30 Ibid.
31 Introduced by the Royal Navy in 1915, the Carley represented a limited advance in the provision of life-saving equipment.

32 The National Archives, ADM 1/19235, Admiralty report of Talbot Committee on naval lifesaving.
33 Jones and Jeffs, 36.
34 Clothier, 68.
35 Clothier, 69–70.
36 Clothier, 68.
37 The National Archives, ADM 53/47434, Admiralty and Ministry of Defence, Navy Department: Ships' logs, *Lucknow*.
38 Imperial War Museum, IMW 220, 'Home on Leave', film of British soldiers returning from the Western Front across the English Channel on leave, early 1916.

Chapter 10

1 Opland and Nyamende, xix.
2 Mkhize, 22–3. The cattle killings were precipitated by a young girl who prophesied in 1856 that if the Xhosa destroyed their herds and crops, their ancestors would rise from the dead and drive out the European colonists.
3 *See* Bevan; Kayle.
4 *See also* South African History Online, 'Conquest of the Eastern Cape 1779–1878', www.sahistory.org.za/topic/conquest-eastern-cape-1779-1878#sthash.fng6LXfQ.dpuf (accessed 26 July 2016).
5 Peires 1987, 43; Stapleton, 383. *See also* Peires 1989 for a detailed account of the cattle killings.
6 Mkhize, 22–3.
7 J Hodgson, 'Fluid assets and fixed investments: 160 years of the Ntsikana tradition' in R Whitaker and E Sienaert (eds), *Oral Tradition and Literacy: Changing Visions of the World*, Natal University Oral Documentation and Research Centre, Durban,1986, quoted in Mkhize, 23.
8 Nyamende, 128; Kirk, 298.
9 Nyamende, 128; Opland and Nyamende, xix.
10 Kirk, 298.
11 Opland and Nyamende, xix.

12 Opland and Nyamende, xiv; Mkhize, 23.
13 Opland and Nyamende, xiv.
14 Odendaal, 5–6.
15 Opland and Nyamende 2008, xiii.
16 Ibid.
17 Opland and Nyamende, xix; Mkhize, 23.
18 Opland and Nyamende, xiv.
19 Ibid.
20 Ibid; Kirk, 298.
21 *See* Davenport.
22 Kirk, 298; Vaughan, 149.
23 *Imbumba* or *mbumba* is a Xhosa word to describe a group with a common cause.
24 Mkhize, 23.
25 Ibid; Mqhayi, quoted in Opland and Nyamende, 406.
26 Opland and Nyamende, xiv; Mkhize, 223.
27 Limb, 237.
28 Opland and Nyamende, xiv.
29 Opland and Nyamende, 407.
30 Mqhayi, quoted in Opland and Nyamende, 408.
31 Ibid.
32 For more about *Umteteli wa bantu*, *see* South African History Online, 'A history of *Umteteli Wabantu*', www.sahistory.org.za/article/history-umteteli-wabantu-1920-1956#sthash.B1Fe4nuo.dpuf (accessed 27 July 2016); Opland and Nyamende, xxviii, refer to the article 'Qalazive, Isi Khumbuzo se Mendi a Bhai', *Umteteli wa bantu,* 10 March 1934, 8.
33 Opland and Nyamende, xxvii–xxxviii.
34 Clothier, 97–8.
35 Grundlingh 2014, 129.
36 Survivor's account from *The Star*, 27 February 1967, quoted in Grundlingh 2014, 128. *See also* Clothier, 56.
37 Grundlingh 2014, 130.
38 *South African Government Gazette* No 25799, 2 December 2003.
39 R Samuel and P Thompson, *The Myths We Live*, Routledge, London, 5, quoted in Grundlingh 2014, 131.
40 Grundlingh 2014, 131.

41 Opland and Nyamende, xiii.

Chapter 11

1 Fawcett, 34.
2 Hacker, 28.
3 A peasant, farmer or agricultural labourer.
4 Howe.
5 Clothier, 14; Xu Guoqi, 39.
6 The National Archives, WO 106/33, Contract for Chinese labourers for France.
7 Clothier, 12; Starling and Lee, 273.
8 *See* Grundlingh 1987; Putkowski.
9 Griffin, 104; Fawcett, 36.
10 Willan, 61–86; Putkowski, 27–9.
11 Fawcett, 37; Putkowski, 11.
12 Starling and Lee, 260.
13 Willan, 73; Clothier, 133–7; Grundlingh 1987, 97; Putkowski, 27.
14 Willan, 73.
15 Grundlingh 1987, 106.
16 Putkowski, 27.
17 Griffin 104, quoting The National Archives, WO 32/5094, 'Proposal for substituting coloured personnel for white in various units in France'.
18 The National Archives, WO 161/2, The historical narrative of the Works Directorate, 2 2, hospitals for coloured labour.
19 Putkowski (pers comm).
20 The National Archives, WO 107/37, Report on the work of labour with the BEF during the war, Cape Boys Labour Battalion, Appendix G: Notes to officers of SANLC.
21 Grundlingh 1987, 112.
22 Grundlingh 1987, 107.
23 Putkowski, 27.
24 National Archives (Pretoria), NTS 9107 16/363.
25 Putkowski, 27.
26 Putkowski, 29.
27 Putkowski, 30.
28 South African National Defence Force Archive (Pretoria), SANDF NTS 9107 12/863 (23 October 1917).
29 Ibid.

30 *See* Commonwealth War Graves Commission casualty database. Available online at http://www.cwgc.org/find-war-dead.aspx (accessed 27 July 2016).

31 Putkowski, 27; Grundlingh 1987, 113; Griffin, 106.

32 National Archives (Pretoria) GG 1681 51/4521, Form of order of commitment to prison, Sam Oliphant (13 February 1918); Starling and Lee, 233.

33 Grundlingh 2014, 87.

34 Grundlingh 1987, 113; National Archives (Pretoria), GG 670 9/93/56.

35 Ibid.

36 The National Archives, WO 95/4115, Lines of communication troops, Native Labour Stationary Hospital; Grundlingh 2014, 89.

37 South African National Defence Force Archive (Pretoria), SANLC Box 2, Daily Orders Medical Section No 3.

38 National Archives (Pretoria), GG 673 9/93/132, Extracts from letters received from certain officers of the SANLC.

39 An alcoholic beverage made from malted millet.

40 National Archives (Pretoria), GG 670 9/93/56, Health report April 1917 (Rouen); December 1917, January 1918.

41 Ibid.

42 South African National Defence Force Archive (Pretoria), DC 1136 (GP 2), DB 1997/Z; National Archives (Pretoria), GG 670 9/93/56 Health report April 1917 (Rouen); December 1917, January 1918.

Chapter 12

1 Walton, 75, quoting *Cape Times* 18 January 1918, 'Native Labour Corps, Premier's message to chiefs and headmen'; National Archives (Pretoria), GG 670 9/93/56, Minute 1921, Prime Minister's Office, 18 December 1917.

2 Cape Archives, I/BIZ 16 362/14/19, Circular No SANLC 10, 3 December 1917.

3 Gleeson, 29.

4 Clothier, 146–7; Grundlingh 1987, 100.

5 Walton 79; Starling and Lee, 228–9.

6 Gleeson, 29.

7 The National Archives, WO 107/37, History of the SANLC: Appendix IIIB: Statistical return respecting natives of the SANLC.

8 Cape Archives, 1/KNT 22 10/1 D, Office of the Chief Magistrate of the Transkeian territories, Umtata. No 778.2/9714 26 July 1917, Native Labour Contingent, circular minute.

9 Willan, 83.

10 For the full text of the petition *see* http://www.anc.org.za/content/petition-king-george-v-south-african-native-national-congress (accessed 11 August 2016).

11 Grundlingh 1982, 12.

12 Grundlingh 1987, 134.

13 Quoted in Grundlingh 1982, 11–12.

14 Grundlingh 1987, 128.

15 Nasson 2007, 165.

16 Grundy 1987, 58.

17 Perry and Perry, 92.

18 Walton, 79.

19 Cape Archives, CMT 3/927 788/2, Native Affairs to all resident magistrates (27 September 1922).

20 Grundy, 60.

21 Gleeson, 45; Willan, 83; Mohlamme, 3.

22 Gleeson, 45–46.

23 Starling and Lee, 234–5.

24 Gleeson, 46.

25 Grundlingh 1982, 8.

26 Cape Archives CMT 3/927/788/2, Transkei Territories General Council Resolution 108 re request medals for SANLC, 14 July 1925.

27 Cape Archives, CMT 3/925/778/2, A K Xabanisa to Chief Magistrate Transkei, 28 December 1919.

Chapter 13

1 UKHO wreck/obstruction record No. 18958: H0121/45 and AUBD 304/56.
2 A dumb vessel, ie one lacking its own propulsion. Normally used for carrying cargo, often between ship and shore, a lighter would usually be towed or pushed by a tug.
3 Magnetometers are commonly used at sea to detect shipwrecks. Towed behind a boat or ship, they can detect the fluctuations in the earth's magnetic field caused by the presence of large amounts of ferrous material on or beneath the seabed.
4 From a transcript of an interview given by Martin Woodward to the author Graham Scott, 2014.
5 Most of the finds recovered from the wreck by Martin Woodward are currently on display as part of his extensive private collection at the Shipwreck Centre and Maritime Museum at Arreton, Isle of Wight.
6 John Buglass, dive logs and pers comm.
7 The 'square' window, a large saloon window from the passenger accommodation, and the previously mentioned shell case were recovered and are now on display at the South African National War Memorial at Delville Wood, France.
8 Various present and former recreational divers interviewed by the authors, pers comm and email.
9 McDonald.
10 One of these windows recovered by a diver from the wreck is on display at the South African National War Museum at Delville Wood, France.
11 Anonymous, nd, 'Recent Diving Activities on the SS *Mendi*', *Elders of Elders* magazine.
12 Pritchard and McDonald, 163 (the information upon which the description is based may be older).
13 Hydrographic surveys carried out by Gardline (UKHO 18958: HI 962).
14 In wire sweeping, a wire is lowered between two ships, which then sweep across the position of a wreck in order to snag it. The wire is then raised in stages on subsequent sweeps until the minimum depth of the wreck is known. This can do damage to parts of a wreck caught by the wire, including the superstructure and masts. Accurate modern methods of surveying mean that wire sweeping is now obsolete.
15 A vaguely defined diving term for objects that divers find attractive to recover.
16 Steven Winstanley, pers comm.
17 Email from Steve of 'Dive Connection, Portsmouth'. No surname given.
18 Dave Wendes, letter of January 2007, and Wendes, 90. (Mr Wendes is a local diving charter vessel operator who is considered an authority on shipwrecks off the Isle of Wight.)
19 Wessex Archaeology 2007.
20 Wessex Archaeology 2008.
21 Mayor and Davies.
22 A steering quadrant is a frame attached to the top of the stock of a rudder. Attaching steering cables to the quadrant enables torque to be applied to a rudder to make it turn.
23 In addition to creating a barrier between salt water and the steel of a ship by repeatedly painting it, sacrificial anodes, also known as galvanic anodes, are used. When iron and steel surfaces come into contact with an electrolyte such as seawater, an electrochemical reaction – corrosion – occurs. Over time, this effectively returns the metal to its natural state as an ore, causing it to disintegrate and lose its structural strength. Large numbers of sacrificial anodes made of more reactive metals and attached to a ship below the waterline are used to disrupt this reaction. They are very effective if used properly, but as the metal of the anodes wastes away because of the reaction, they have to be replaced at regular intervals. Once a

ship has sunk, they rapidly become exhausted. Attempts by archaeologists to protect iron-and-steel shipwrecks using anodes have generally failed, owing to the costs and long-term effort involved in maintaining the protection.

24 Steven Winstanley, pers comm.

25 Of BSAC, the British Sub-Aqua Club.

26 The markings on the base of the cartridge indicated to John Buglass that it had been fired once and reloaded with cordite, but that it had then been unloaded.

27 These can be seen at the Shipwreck Centre and Maritime Museum at Arreton, Isle of Wight.

28 The outer walls of the superstructure, the technical term being 'boundary bulkheads'.

29 HMSO, 162. (Facsimile reprint of four 1919 HMSO publications, including *British Merchant Shipping [Losses]*). The figures given in this publication are losses due to war hazards only and have not been updated to take into account subsequent corrections and research.

30 Maw, 1.

31 Scott.

32 Wise and Baron, 75–80. A report in *The Times* in September 1915 published an Admiralty casualty list of 864 missing, believed drowned.

33 Viduka, 154–68.

34 Wessex Archaeology, 2007.

35 *Sydney Morning Herald*, 17 September 1918.

36 Rogers, Introductory.

Chapter 14

1 Former Prime Minister David Cameron in a speech at the Imperial War Museum on First World War centenary plans, 11 October 2012. Available online at https://www.gov.uk/government/speeches/speech-at-imperial-war-museum-on-first-world-war-centenary-plans (accessed 26 July 2016).

References

Anonymous nd 'Recent Diving Activities on the SS *Mendi*'. *Elders of Elders* magazine

Bevan, D 1972 *Drums of the Birkenhead*. New York: Larson Publications

Buxton, S 1924 *General Botha*. London: Murray

Clothier, N 1987 *Black Valour: The South African Native Labour Contingent, 1916–1918, and the sinking of the* Mendi. Pietermaritzburg: University of Natal Press

Collyer, J J 1937 *The Campaign in German South West Africa 1914–1915*. Pretoria: Government Printer

Collyer, J J 1939 *The South Africans with General Smuts in German East Africa, 1916*. Pretoria: Government Printer

Davenport, T R H 1966 *The Afrikaner Bond: The History of a South African Political Party, 1880–1911*. Cape Town: Oxford University Press

Elder Dempster & Co Ltd 1921 *The Elder Dempster Fleet in the War, 1914–1918*. Liverpool: Elder Dempster & Co Ltd

Elgood, P G 1924 *Egypt and the Army*. Oxford: Oxford University Press

Farrow, E S 1895 *Farrow's Military Encyclopedia*, Military-Naval Publishing Company

Fawcett, B C 2000 'Chinese Labour Corps in France 1917–1921'. *Journal of the Hong Kong Branch of the Royal Asiatic Society*, **40**, 33–111

Gleeson, I 1994 *The Unknown Force: Black, Indian and Coloured Soldiers Through Two World Wars*. Rivonia: Ashanti

Grace's Guide to British Industrial History 1932 *A Shipbuilding History 1750–1932*. Glasgow: Alexander Stephen & Sons

Greenway, A 2009 *Cargo Liners: An Illustrated History*. Barnsley: Seaforth Publishing Ltd

Griffin, N J 1976 'Britain's Chinese Labor Corps in World War I'. *Military Affairs*, **40**:3, October 1976, 102–8

Griffiths, D 1997 *Steam at Sea: Two Centuries of Steam-powered Ships*. London: Conway Maritime Press

Grundlingh, A 1982 'Black men in a white man's war: the impact of the First World War on South African blacks'. Unpublished seminar paper, University of Witwatersrand, African Studies Institute

Grundlingh, A 1987 *Fighting Their Own War: South African Blacks and the First World War*. Johannesburg: Ravan Press

Grundlingh, A 2014 *War and Society, Participation and Remembrance: South African Black and Coloured Troops in the First World War, 1914–1918*. Stellenbosch: Sun Press

Grundy, K W 1983 *Soldiers Without Politics: Blacks in the South African Armed Forces*, Perspective on Southern Africa 33. Berkeley: University of California Press

Hacker, B C 2014 'White man's war, coloured man's labour: working for the British Army on the Western Front'. *Itinerio* **38**:3, 27–44

Hallifax, S 2010 'Over by Christmas: British popular opinion and the short war in 1914'. *First World War Studies*, **1**:2, 103–21

Havinden, M and Meredith, D 1993 *Colonialism and Development: Britain and its Tropical Colonies, 1850–1960*. London and New York: Routledge

HMSO 1988 *British Vessels lost at Sea 1914–1918*. Cambridge: Patrick Stephens Ltd

Howe, G 2011 *A White Man's War? World War One and the West Indies*. Available online at http://www.bbc.co.uk/history/worldwars/wwone/west_indies_01.shtml (accessed 19 February 2016)

Jones, S R and T M Jeffs 1991 'Near-surface sea temperatures in coastal waters of the North Sea, English Channel and Irish Sea'. MAFF Fisheries Research Data Report No. 24.

Kayle, A 1990 *Salvage of the Birkenhead*. Johannesburg: Southern Book Publishers

Killingray, D 1989 'Labour exploitation for military campaigns in British Colonial Africa 1870–1945'. *Journal of Contemporary History*, **24**:3, 483–501

Killingray, D 2001 'African voices from the two world wars'. *Historical Research*, **74**:186, 425–43

Kirk, J F 1991 'Race, class, liberalism, and segregation: the 1883 Native Strangers' Location Bill in Port Elizabeth, South Africa'. *International Journal of African Historical Studies*, **24**:2, 293–321

Klein, D nd *With the Chinks*. Uckfield and London: Naval & Military Press and Imperial War Museum.

Limb, P 2010 *The ANC's Early Years*. Pretoria: UNISA Press

Lugard, Lord F D 1922 *The Dual Mandate in British Tropical Africa*. London and Edinburgh: W Blackwood & Sons

Marti S nd 'Dominions' Military Relationship to Great Britain 1902–1914 (British Dominions)', International Encyclopedia of the First World War. Available online at http://encyclopedia.1914-1918-online.net/article/dominions_military_relationship_to_great_

britain_1902-1914_british_dominions (accessed 26 July 2016)

Maw, N 1999 *World War One Channel Wrecks: Vessels Lost in the English Channel 1914–1918*. Hampton: Underwater World Publications

Mayor, A and Davies, M 2011 'SS *Mendi*'. BSAC *SCUBA* magazine, December 2011, 57–63

McDonald, K 1989 'The 20-Minute Tragedy'. *Diver* magazine, May 1989

Mkhize, K 2008 'Carrying the Cross: Isaac William(s) Wauchope's *Ingcamango Ebunzimeni*'. MA thesis, University of the Witwatersrand, Department of African Literature

Mohlamme, J S 1995 'Soldiers without reward: Africans in South Africa's wars'. *Journal of the South African Military History Society*, **10**:1, 1–10

Mostert, N 1992 *Frontiers: The Epic of South Africa's Creation and the Tragedy of the Xhosa People*. New York: Knopf

Nasson, B 2004 'Why they fought: black Cape colonists and Imperial wars, 1899–1918'. *International Journal of African Historical Studies*, **37**:1, 55–70

Nasson, B 2007 *Springboks on the Somme: South Africa in the Great War 1914–1918*. Johannesburg: Penguin

Nasson, B 2014 *WWI and the People of South Africa*. Cape Town: Tafelberg

Nyamende, M A 2000 'The Life and Works of Isaac William(s) Wauchope'. Unpublished PhD thesis, University of Cape Town

Odendaal, A 1984 *Vukani Bantu! The Beginnings of Black Protest Politics in South Africa to 1912*. Cape Town: David Philip

Opland, J and Nyamende, M A (eds) 2008 *Isaac Williams Wauchope: Selected Writings, 1874–1916*. Cape Town: Van Riebeeck Society

Paterson, H 2004 'First Allied victory: the South African campaign in German South-West Africa, 1914–1915'.

Journal of the South African Military History Society, **13**:2, 1–9

Peires, J B 1987 'The central beliefs of the Xhosa cattle-killing'. *Journal of African History*, **28**, 43–63

Peires, J B 1989 *The Dead Will Arise: Nongqawuse and the Great Xhosa Cattle-killing Movement of 1856–7*. Johannesburg: Ravan Press

Peregrino, F Z S 1917 *His Majesty's Black Labourers: A Treatise on the Camp Life of the SANLC*. Cape Town: Cape Times

Perry, J and Perry, C (eds) 1975 *A Chief is a Chief by the People*. Oxford: Oxford University Press

Plaatje, S T 1916 *Native Life in South Africa, Before and Since the European War and the Boer Rebellion*. London: P S King & Son Ltd

Pritchard, M and McDonald, K 2001 *Dive Wight and Hampshire*. Hampton: Underwater World Publications

Putkowski, J 1998 *British Army Mutineers 1914–1922*. London: Francis Boutle

Rogers, Colonel H C B 1963 *Imperial Services Library Volume VII: Troopships and Their History*. London: Seeley Service & Co Ltd

Samson, A 2006 *Britain, South Africa and the East African Campaign, 1914–1918: The Union Comes of Age*. London and New York: Tauris Academic Studies

Savage D, and J Forbes Munro 1966 'Carrier Corps recruitment in the British East Africa Protectorate: 1914–1918', *The Journal of African History*, **7**:2, 313–432

Scott, R N 2012 *Many Were Held by the Sea: The Tragic Sinking of HMS Otranto*. Lanham, Maryland: Rowman & Littlefield

Slaven, A 1993 'Shipbuilding in Nineteenth-Century Scotland' *in* S Ville (ed) *Shipbuilding in the United Kingdom in the Nineteenth Century: A Regional Approach* (Research in Maritime History **4**). St John's, Newfoundland: International Maritime History Economic History Association/Trustees of the National Museums and Galleries on Merseyside

South African Government Gazette No 25799, 2 December 2003, 4–6

South African History Online, 'Conquest of the Eastern Cape 1779–1878'. http://www.sahistory.org.za/topic/conquest-eastern-cape-1779-1878#sthash.fng6LXfQ.dpuf (accessed 26 July 2016)

Starling, J and Lee, I 2009 *No Labour, No Battle: Military Labour During the First World War*. Stroud: Spellmount

Stapleton, T J 1991 '"They no longer care for their chiefs": Another look at the Xhosa cattle-killing of 1856–1857'. *International Journal of African Historical Studies*, **24**:2, 383–92

Stuart, J 1913 *A History of the Zulu Rebellion 1906 and of Dinizulu's Arrest, Trial and Expatriation*. London: Macmillan & Co

Swart, S 1998 'A Boer and his gun and his wife are three things always together: Republican masculinity and the 1914 rebellion'. *Journal of Southern African Studies* **24**:4, 737–51

The Long, Long Trail 1996 'The labour corps of 1917–1918'. Available online at http://www.longlongtrail.co.uk/army/regiments-and-corps/the-labour-corps-of-1917-1918/ (accessed 27 July 2016)

The Western Front Association 2008 'The British pioneer battalions and labour corps on the Western Front in the Great War'. Available online at http://www.westernfrontassociation.com/the-great-war/great-war-on-land/general-interest/810-labour-corps-pionners.html#sthash.uv13BVQq.dpbs (accessed 27 July 2016)

Truman C T 2015 'The Dominions and World War One'. Available online at http://www.historylearningsite.co.uk/world-war-one/the-dominions-and-world-war-one/ (accessed 26 July 2016)

Turrell, R 1984 'Kimberley's model compounds'. *Journal of African History*, **25**:1, 59–75

Vaughan, M 2006 'Africa and the Birth of the Modern World', *Transactions of the Royal Historical Society* **16**, 143–62. Cambridge: Cambridge University Press

Viduka, A 2015 'An Overview of Australia's World War I Underwater Cultural Heritage 1914–1924 and Observations on Changing National Expectations to Commemoration'. *Underwater Cultural Heritage from World War I: Proceedings of the Scientific Conference on the Occasion of the Centenary of World War I, Bruges, Belgium, 26 & 27 June 2014,* UNESCO, 154–68

Walton, S 2015 'The *Mendi* and the South African Native Labour Corps'. Unpublished research report for the South Africa Heritage Resources Agency

Warwick, P 1983 *Black People and the South African War 1899–1902*. Cambridge University Press, Cambridge

Wendes, D 2006 *South Coast Shipwrecks off East Dorset and Wight*. Self-published

Wessex Archaeology 2007 'SS *Mendi* archaeological desk-based assessment'. Unpublished report, ref. 64441.01. Available online at http://www.wessexarch.co.uk/files/projects/ss-Mendi/ssMendiReport.pdf (accessed 25 July 2016)

Wessex Archaeology 2008 'SS *Mendi* Geophysical Survey: Data Processing and Assessment'. Available online at http://www.wessexarch.co.uk/projects/marine/eh/ssmendi/reports/geophysical-assessment-report (accessed 26 July 2016)

Willan, B P 1978 'The South African Native Labour Contingent, 1916–1918'. *Journal of African History*, **19**:1, 61–86

Wise, J E and Baron, S 2004 *Soldiers Lost at Sea: A Chronicle of Troopship Disasters*. Annapolis, MD: Naval Institute Press

Worden, N 2007 *The Making of Modern South Africa*. Oxford: Blackwell

Xu Guoqi 2011 *Strangers on the Western Front: Chinese workers in the Great War*. Cambridge, MA: Harvard University Press

Young, M 2000 *Army Service Corps 1902–1918*. Barnsley: Pen and Sword

Acknowledgements

The writing of this book would have been impossible without the help of a host of people who have given freely and generously of their knowledge, time and advice. It is impossible to list everyone who has contributed, but you know who you are. To you all – thank you. Without your support, encouragement and generosity it is unlikely that this book will have been written.

We must, acknowledge the following special debts.

- Antony Firth, for encouraging and supporting a germ of an idea ten years ago;
- Ian Oxley, Mark Dunkley and Rachel Hasted of Historic England and Jonathan Sharfman of the South African Heritage Resources Agency for seeing its merit and providing the funding to allow the idea to be realised;
- Current and former colleagues at Wessex Archaeology and the South African Heritage Resources Agency who have supported this publication or been involved in archaeological and educational work on the *Mendi* including, Toby Gane, Pippa Bradley, Stephanie Arnott, Gemma Ingason, Louise Tizzard, Will and Kitty Foster, Karen Nichols, Peta Knott and Sarah Walton;
- The late Norman Clothier and Albert Grundlingh, whose research for the first major works on the loss of the *Mendi* and history of the South African Native Labour Corps respectively, have informed this book;
- Pamela and Donald Veysie for sharing reminiscences and the memoir of Pam's grandfather, Captain Lewis Herslet of the SANLC;
- The descendants of Sergeant Robert MacTavish for access to the family archive;
- Martin Woodward, discoverer of the wreck of the *Mendi*, for his recollections and access to his collection of artefacts;
- John Buglass, Keith Rimes and Dave Wendes for sharing their recollections of and research into the wreck;
- Martin Davies, underwater photographer, for access to his archive of photographs of the wreck;
- Marion Edmunds and Shawn Sobers whose films on the *Mendi* have been a source of inspiration and information about the wreck;

- The *We Die Like Brothers* exhibition team, in particular Susan Hayward and Thapedi Masanabo, for access to their research;
- South African Deputy President Cyril Ramaphosa, who was very supportive of the *We Die Like Brothers* project;
- Former Prime Minister David Cameron for understanding the significance of the *Mendi* and for the encouragement he has provided to those seeking to communicate that importance to the public; and
- The publication team at Historic England for their enthusiasm and professional guidance as we wrote this book.

Lastly, to our respective partners, Gail Euston-Brown and Susan Hayward and Amy and Rachel Gribble: Thank you for sharing us over the past ten years with the men of the *Mendi* and the SANLC and with the wreck of a ship lying in quiet obscurity in the cold waters of the English Channel.

Index